The Nuremberg rallies

D1191137

The Nuremberg rallies

Alan Wykes

Editor-in-Chief: Barrie Pitt
Art Director: Peter Dunbar

Military Consultant: Sir Basil Liddell Hart
Picture Editor: Robert Hunt

Executive Editor: David Mason
Designer: Sarah Kingham
Special Drawings: John Batchelor
Cartographer: Richard Natkiel
Cover: Denis Piper
Research Assistant: Yvonne Marsh

Ballantine Books Inc.
101 Fifth Avenue New York NY 10003

Contents

Pageantry of power

Introduction by Barrie Pitt

No-one in history understood the basic principles of mass persuasion better than Hitler, and no organisation expended more labour and material in perfecting and using its techniques than did the Nazi Party during its turbulent and vicious life. And in the astounding spectacles which became known as the Nuremberg Rallies, every art, subterfuge and contrivance was employed to hammer into the spectators and participants the message that National Socialism was the only religion and Hitler its God, and the art of propaganda – if art it is – reached its zenith.

Not all the rallies were, in fact, held at Nuremberg. The first was held in Munich and the third – ironically in view of the Nazi intentions towards the Government which bore its name – in Weimar, but Nuremberg was the scene for the most spectacular and the most significant, and was indeed historically fitted for the nursery of any creed which preached and practiced violent anti-semitism. It was also conveniently at the junction of seven main railway lines along which in due course the special trains could bring the labour corps, the SS troops, the Hitler youths and eventually the spectators. Hitler himself arrived last, on one incredible occasion by plane which came into view of the massed and devoted millions at the very moment that day-long clouds parted and the sun broke through. Expert organiser though Dr Göbbels undoubtedly was, he was not accorded responsibility for that.

In fact it was not Göbbels, but the infamous Julius Streicher who was responsible for both the original decision to hold the rallies at Nuremberg and for the admirable efficiency

with which they were organised and controlled, and it is this aspect of the rallies which puzzles the reader now, and some of the spectators thirty and more years ago. Hitler could hardly carry on a coherent conversation with a single person, let alone argue a case with an intelligent one; after the war and while awaiting trial for War Crimes, Julius Streicher was subjected to intelligence tests which revealed him as possessing the brain and reasoning power of a moron; yet between them these two men organised pageants which necessitated the marshalling, equipping, feeding and then dispersal of hundreds of thousands of men, women and children, not to speak of the details of the pageantry in which they all took part. Certainly in the later rallies they had at their disposal the not inconsiderable talents of Dr Göbbels, together of course with those of thousands of other gifted individuals – but to some extent this heightens the mystery; how could people capable of such artistry as was exhibited and of such organising ability as was evident, accept the turgid philosophy which was the mainspring of the event?

It is one of the many virtues of this book that Alan Wykes has gone as far as anyone ever can to explain this curious phenomenon, to exhibit this odd German dichotomy of behaviour which can produce a marvel of foresight, organisation and either scientific or artistic imagination, all devoted to an entirely worthless cause.

And National Socialism as practiced by Hitler was worse than worthless; it was one of the most evil manifestations of megalomania known to history.

'Greater Germany'

The last and biggest of the Nazi rallies was held at Nuremberg from 5th to 12th September 1938. Its theme was 'Greater Germany'. Well before the opening day the spirit of greater Germany could be seen at unpredictable hours stalking through the streets in the person of *Gauleiter* Julius Streicher. Attended by two evil-looking henchmen, he carried a whip which he cracked continuously. People edged into the gutter at his approach. He was said to be looking

for Jews, clearing the town for the Führer, like the falconers of medieval times who led the emperor's procession to clear the rats from his path.

By 1938 there were of course no Jews in Nuremberg; or if there were they must have been remarkably adept at evading the machinations of the secret police. But with Streicher habits died hard. The absence of the object of his pathological hatred in no way lessened his malevolence. A pervert, pornographer, and criminal sadist he could, and did, direct these talents in many directions. With Willy Liebel, the mayor, he was responsible for the exploitation and perversion of the town's historical and cultural assets, their transformation into the epitome of Nazism.

Streicher had been, in the early 1920s, leader of an anti-Semitic party in Nuremberg that had rivalled the Nazis for a time; and as a reward for

Sieg Heil!

throwing in his hand with Hitler had been made *Gauleiter* – that is, Party leader in the area.

'He had,' said Hitler in *Mein Kampf*, 'a sacred conviction of the mission and future of his own movement. As soon, however, as the superior strength and stronger growth of the National Socialist German Labour Party became clear and unquestionable to his mind he gave up his work in the German Socialist Party and called upon his followers to fall into line with the National Socialist German Labour Party, which had come out victorious from the mutual contest, and carry on the fight within its ranks for the common cause. The decision was personally a difficult one for him, but it showed a profound sense of honesty.'

Streicher's sacred conviction and profound honesty having gained him exactly the position that gave full scope to his limited intellect and unlimited sadism, he put it to Hitler that Nuremberg was the ideal venue for the party congress. 'The National Socialist life breathes in the ancient walls and gable and moat,' he said. That was in 1923. In 1938 what he had said as a wheedling phrase had become an accomplished fact. There was an emanation of evil from the town. Its gingerbread architecture, narrow streets and open markets gave off 'the stench of the Nazi heart', according to one London newspaper correspondent; 'the thousands of Nazi banners flutter in a miasma of evil intent and the endless lines of tents are stuffed with the brutality of storm troopers and secret police.' Streicher, striding through the town with his aides and his whip, turning out of his way to make one of his frequent visits to the medieval torture chamber beneath the Rathaus, may well have been pleased with the long-term results of his direction of Party affairs in Nuremberg.

As July and August passed and the first day of the rally approached, an intense but orderly activity electrified the town. Hundreds of trains and convoys of lorries brought men, supplies and weapons. Experts with clip-boards and stopwatches worked out precise timings for motorcades and measurements for processional routes. In the nine camps in the environs of the town thousands of tents were erected in faultless lines, the pathways between them paved with concrete. In the stadia scaffolders raised huge neon-lit eagles and serried rows of flagstaffs from the tops of which broke hundreds of Nazi banners. Generators, floodlights, latrines, kitchens and canteens appeared as if by magic. At the Rathaus vendors of food, drink and novelty souvenirs lined up for licences. Great batteries of arc lights and searchlights were moved into position. Bunches of mushroom-shaped loudspeakers bloomed like fungus upon steel towers. By day and night the sound of hammers, drills, and excavators went on. Parties of organizers filled the hotels and administrative buildings. Corps of workmen were transported or marched about the town and beneath their hands hall and theatre and arena were transformed into settings for speeches, exhibitions, and demonstrations. To the Nurembergers it was familiar, the annual orgasm of the Party. They flung up their arms in the Nazi salute and stood aside for *Gauleiter* Streicher. Greater Germany surrounded them; they could not have been more lasciviously pleased.

The representatives of the world's press – more than 700 of them – unaccustomed to regimentation, arrived by their varied routes and methods, according to their influence and the angles of the congress they wanted to cover. Dr Otto Dietrich, the Reich press chief, had arranged a reception for them immediately prior to Hitler's arrival at the Rathaus on the afternoon of 5th September. But they were pouring into the town days before that. Like everyone else they were impressed by the effects, the organiza-

The march through Nuremberg

Above: 'Germany awake!'
Right: Göring, Wagnerian in flowing
cape, arrives at the rally

tion. They could hardly fail to be.
Four years earlier William Shirer,
one of the greatest of them, had
written, in what would later be called
his Berlin Diary:

'Like a Roman emperor Hitler rode
into this medieval town . . . past solid
phalanxes of wildly cheering Nazis
who packed the narrow streets that
once saw Hans Sachs and the *Meister-*
singer. Tens of thousands of swastika
fags blot out the Gothic beauties of
the place, the facades of the old
houses, the gabled roofs. The streets,
hardly wider than alleys, are a sea
of brown and black uniforms . . . About
ten o'clock tonight I got caught in a
mob of ten thousand hysterics who
jammed the moat in front of Hitler's
hotel, shouting: "We want our
Führer". I was a little shocked at
the faces, especially those of the

women, when Hitler finally appeared on the balcony for a moment. They reminded me of the crazed expressions I saw once in . . . Louisiana on the faces of some Holy Rollers . . . They looked up at him as if he were a Messiah, their faces transformed into something positively inhuman.'

Many of the press men, the veterans, had covered all the congresses and each year made of their stories a kind of serial which now approached a climax. The world was waiting for Greater Germany and for her Messiah to reveal his hand. Six months earlier he had marched his troops across the border and bloodlessly acquired Austria, his native land, as the first of his territorial conquests. Now the Sudetenland affair was moving toward its climax. 'This miserable pygmy race of Czechs,' as Göring was to call them, 'without culture, is oppressing a cultured people and behind it is Moscow and the eternal mask of the Jew devil.' What, at this 1938 congress, would Hitler say on the last day of

the rally a week hence? The reporters gathered in conclaves, voiced the opinions of London, Rome, New York, Paris. They drank in bars, sent their cables, waited for Dr Dietrich to give them the prefabricated Nazi story.

Surprisingly, Dietrich this year was all sweetness and light. His customary swingeing attack on 'the Jew-inspired so-called freedom of the press' was no more than a glancing blow. Extravagant phrases inflated the marvels of the German economy, the strength of the armed forces, the endlessness of the stores of grain ('reserves for the whole nation for four years'), the utter happiness of the German people in the stability of the Nazi régime. One might justly have said of his speech, as Churchill said of an outpouring of Anthony Eden's, that it contained every cliché in the repertoire except God is Love and Please Adjust Your Dress Before Leaving. The reporters sat cynically listening and preparing their questions. What about the Czechs and the Sudeten

Germans? What if England marched? Daladier and Gamelin?

Dietrich waggishly replied that they must all wait and see and he hoped they had all taken full note of the military strength revealed in the display put on ten days before in Berlin. Continuing waggish, he winked and said that as journalists they would all realize that though the display was ostensibly put on for the benefit of Admiral Horthy, the Regent of Hungary, it was a show of strength to the world.

'And which part of the world is to feel it first?' *Le Matin* asked.

The reception broke up without answers having been given to any of the important questions except in terms of euphemism and rodomontade. The journalists took up their stations for the arrival of Hitler – or, if they were familiar with that particular scene, bustled to other parts of the town where casual comments or mood-pieces could be sought for.

In the streets and squares the Shirer scene was reliving itself in a doubly frenzied and amplified form. As the time drew nearer for the Führer's arrival the crowds began to sing – the *Horst Wessel* song, *Deutschland*, the *Badenweiler* march. It was as if the tunes rose in pre-determined order from a million throats conducted by an invisible hand. Between them came the chanted sacred words *Sieg Heil! Hitler, Vaterland*, beginning as a low mutter and growing to a rhythmic roar.

In the Luitpoldhain, the Zeppelinwiese, the Congress Hall, the fair grounds, the Opera House, the theatres, the Kulturvereinshaus, the Rathaus, the banners and Klieg lights were suspended over vast areas of seats, concrete, grass. The surfaced roads dividing thousands of tents on the fringe of the town were all named for dead or heroic party members, and at every intersection was a hoarding

Hitler addresses the multitude at the Zeppelinwiese

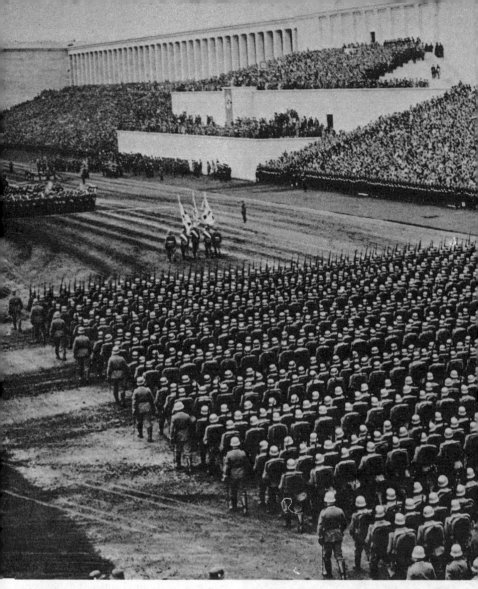

displaying the camp rules. Nobody could walk more than twenty yards without being visually reminded by an *Achtung!* that all orders were to be obeyed immediately, that there was to be no smoking in the tents, that tattoo would be sounded at 22.00 hours and that everyone would be in bed and silent by 22.30, that no one would leave without a pass or return without reporting, that swimming in rivers and walking in woods was forbidden. And so on. There was a continual stream of earnest readers of the hoardings. 'No doubt,' the *Star* man observed, 'they are watching for new rules by which they may achieve strength through joy. In Britain many surreptitious *graffiti* would have been added; but here ironic comment, like walking through the woods, is of course forbidden and would doubtless

be rewarded by court-martial and death at dawn, no less.'

Every aspect of organization in fact worked faultlessly. No eventualities were left uncovered. At one extreme rules existed for the disposal of fallen thunderbolts; at the other for the prevention of the blocking of urinals. Everything was coded, documented, paragraphed. 'Just like forms from the English Civil Service,' said

The march past the Führer

the *Mirror* sourly, 'except that here the words are longer and louder and the Germans understand them.'

It was not surprising that Hitler's arrival was perfectly timed, nor that five minutes before his train steamed into the station the roar of the crowds ceased as if cut by a switch. Complete silence enveloped the town. Nothing moved but the thousands of banners ruffled fitfully by the breeze, and the symbolic torch, the 'eternal flame' burning brightly in the Zeppelinwiese. The Führer might have been entering a dead place.

But as he left the station, flanked by Heinrich Himmler and Rudolf Hess, the tumult broke out again. It ran like an electric current through the streets, the switch now in reverse, the signal booming from the tannoys: 'The Führer has arrived'.

The immense five-ton car, twenty feet long and with half-inch armoured glass windows, awaited him. As Shirer had observed, he drove like a Roman emperor through the town – perhaps even with a potential assassin lurking in the crowd, a plot for his downfall already in embryo. Who can tell?

At the Rathaus the throng was briefly silent again before the fanfares sounded and the bands played him in. Mayor Liebel spoke the platitude of welcome. The reporters could have noted them without even listening; but the public address system carried every word into every corner; there was no escape. This year, however, there was something to follow – a presentation.

It was not the first of its kind. In 1934, when Hitler had been Chancellor for only a year – and self-appointed at that – he had presented himself with copies of the crown, orb and sceptre that had been the royal insignia of the emperor Charlemagne. He had of course done this in the name of the German people – 'I accept these into my keeping on behalf of the glorious Fatherland' – but ownership of them was no more than a symbol of his wild lust for power, whatever he might blather about the expression of the bond between the First Empire and the Third Reich. Although a complete materialist, personal possessions of value did not attract him; and he spent his life kicking at the class system that belonged to monarchic rule. But the symbols of domination – these were the trappings of his lust.

Now, six months after marching into Austria, he had acquired more baubles. The crown jewels of the Habsburg monarchy included some of the pieces made for the 15th-century German King Frederick III. Frederick was a lapidarian as well as an alchemist and astrologer and, like Hitler, had megalomaniac designs for the conquest of other nations. But he never achieved any conquests – indeed, he was bullied to such an extent by Matthias of Hungary and other minor kings that on his death in 1493, after more than fifty years of ineffective rule he was still only a refugee from his own capital, Vienna, where Matthias held sway over the embryo Austro-Hungarian empire. However, Frederick never ceased to cherish his grandiose designs, and the gold settings for his immense collection of gems were incised with the monogram AEIOU, *Austriae est imperare orbi universo* ('It is for Austria to rule the world').

The phrase delighted Hitler. Was he not Austrian himself? Had he not restored to Germany the former heart of her great empire? The *anschluss* accomplished, he lost no time in commissioning copies of the pieces; and it was these that were to be 'presented' to him by Mayor Liebel.

The press did not fail to latch on to the significance of this symbolic gesture. It was described variously as 'a stroke of impertinent self-importance', 'typical power-lust expressed in cheap melodrama', 'Imperialism run riot', 'a tangible compensation for the humiliation Hitler suffered when forced to abandon his plans for the annexation of Czecho-Slovakia' (in the previous May) and 'the childish acquisition of toys by a dangerous upstart'.

They were not phrases likely to please Hitler; nor did they. But he pretended to consider them irrelevant and to treat them with contempt. His decision as to Czecho-Slovakia had

The display flight over the arena

18

been made on 30th May, a week after the other European powers had forced him to climb down: 'It is my unalterable decision to smash Czecho-Slovakia by military action in the near future. It is the business of the political leadership to bring about the suitable moment from a political and military point of view.' The suitable moment had been brought about by

Storm troopers: a contingent from East Germany

Konrad Henlein, leader of the Sudetan Germans in Czecho-Slovakia, who had cunningly contrived such a situation of discontent that Hitler's plan for the destruction of the Czech state under the usual guise of intervention to prevent civil war had moved as if on well oiled wheels toward its climax, and the world now waited for his speech at the end of the rally – a speech that would indicate a move toward either peace or war. Hitler could afford to ignore the wounding

remarks of the foreign press about baubles and childishness. His conceit was enormous and it had been pricked. But he suppressed his anger. The press could wait till the 12th for the lash of his tongue.

After the presentation of the jewels, which Hitler of course again accepted 'on behalf of the German people', there were no further surprises. The rally was officially opened the next day by Rudolf Hess, with Streicher following with his customary veno-

mous diatribe against Jews and Marxists. Hitler reviewed the flags of the Hitler Youth and an exhibition designed to prepare the German people for war with Russia was opened. It was called 'The Struggle in the East' and showed Russia as an evil aggressor and western Europe (meaning Germany) as struggling for *lebensraum* and cultural freedom. Cultural freedom of the German stamp was expressed in the evening at the Opera House, where Dr Göbbels announced the winners of the National Prizes, which Hitler had instituted in place of the Nobel Prizes, which Germans were forbidden to accept. The highlight of this 'cultural' assembly was a speech by Hitler in which he denounced the 'misinter-pretations of international Jewry' and the uselessness of religion.

'Our National Socialist architects,' he said, 'cannot be expected to design a church, any more than one could conceive a Gothic stadium. They cannot design a religious building because such a building is incom-patible with the National Socialist spirit. We do not need religious buildings, we need parade grounds. To our mind, there is nothing to be gained from religious buildings. The only standard for art is whether it appeals to mankind's sense of the beautiful, the healthy, and the natural. And that is wholly against the Jewish belief that decadent intellectuals alone are entitled to set up standards.'

Needless to say, no such belief, Jewish or otherwise, existed; nor, if it had, would it have had any connection with religion. Hitler's speeches, like his thoughts and aphorisms, were always stuffed with *non sequiturs*. He twisted ideas as he twisted facts, to suit a particular point he wanted to make at a given moment. Thus, when next day he gave a reception for the ambassadors of foreign nations, he was able to say – according to François-Poincet of France 'with the deepest sincerity' – 'I trust that no mother will ever have cause to weep

21

in consequence of any action of mine.' That reception was held immediately after Hitler had had a private interview with Konrad Henlein and despatched him to the Sudetenland to set in motion the machinery for grinding the forces of 'the despicable Czechs' into the dust.

Throughout the week the customary pattern of the rallies was followed. 'Display after display,' said the *New York Times*, 'each bigger and more astonishingly beautiful than ever before,' punctuated by speeches, added the *Chronicle*, 'that grow ever longer and never less hideously threatening.'

Indeed the displays were astonishing. The British ambassador, Sir Nevile Henderson, said of them: 'I spent six years in St Petersburg before the war in the best days of the old Russian ballet, but for grandiose beauty I have never seen a ballet to compare with it'. There were displays by the Hitler Youth, the Labour Corps, the armed forces, the Storm Troops, athletes, women. To witness them was to be hypnotized by power, music, movement, light, drama. It was impossible not to have the emotions seized and twisted by the sunlight glinting on the 40,000 spades of the Labour Corps, the faultless marching of countless thousands of troops, the torches smoking in the huge arenas beneath canopies of searchlights, the massed bands and the roar of the crowds.'

As for the speeches, they ran in time from the few minutes of Hess's opening address to the two-hour-plus set pieces of Göring and Hitler. Ranting and raving were the keynotes of both the fat Field-Marshal's and the Chancellor's sermons. Göbbels' was no less deadly with venom but he chose less crude phrases. Ministers of Agriculture (Walther Darré), Justice (Hans Frank), and Engineering (Fritz Todt) fed their audiences with endless statistics. Mrs Scholtz-Klink, leader of the Party women, announced that

The banners of youth

no German girl would get any kind of paid job until she had given the state a year of voluntary unpaid service. 'This is the same as saying,' wrote Pembroke Stephens of the *Daily Express*, ' "Right: I call for volunteers – you, you and you".'

Hitler's final speech on the last night of the rally was as always timed for eight o'clock. (There was of course a reason: it shall be revealed.) Three nights earlier he had summoned a secret military conference at which he had complained that the plans of the army Commander-in-Chief, Field-Marshal von Brauchitsch, were over-cautious. 'My aim is to drive straight through to Prague and leave the Czech army in the rear. And this is to be done on 30th September.' With only eighteen days to go before he invaded Czecho-Slovakia, and confident that he had now persuaded Brauchitsch to mount a full-scale *blitzkreig*, he had no need to pull his punches in his speech. Nor did he.

His main attack was on President Benes, for whom his personal hatred was unremittingly bitter. But the Czech state (the symbol of Versailles), President Woodrow Wilson, the viciousness of the Czech soldiers' attacks on Sudeten Germans, and Britain's policy in Palestine were all subjected to his blistering fury.

'I am in no way willing that here in the heart of Germany a second Palestine should be permitted to arise. The poor Arabs are defenceless and deserted. The Germans in Czecho-Slovakia are neither defenceless nor are they deserted, and people should take notice of that fact.'

The words can be read calmly enough; but delivered as only Hitler could deliver them, in the blaze cast by the great kliegs and the tent of searchlights piercing the night sky, they were terrifying.

'At every pause,' says Alan Bullock in *Hitler: a Study in Tyranny*, 'the deep baying of the huge crowd gathered under the stars, and the roar of "*Sieg Heil! Sieg Heil! Sieg Heil!*" supplied a

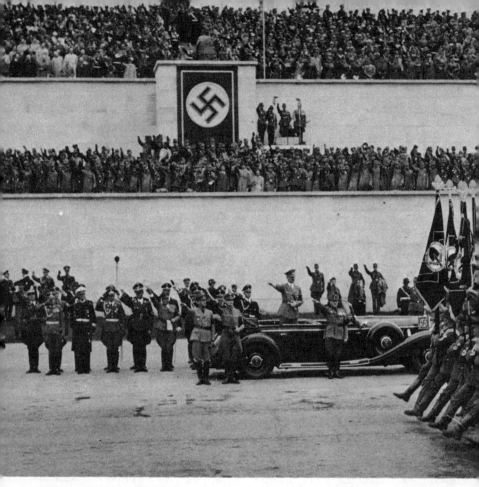

Above: Goose-step past the Führer
Right: Church and state: the
Liebfrauenkirche and the Führer

sinister background. At last the one-time agitator of the Munich beer-halls had the world for audience.'

The world's newspapers responded with the most lengthy coverage of the speech – often verbatim in translation. They could not have played into Hitler's hands more satisfactorily. To know that almost every nation hung upon his words was complete satiety for his colossal conceit – quite apart from the boost given to his megalomania by the knowledge that, in spite of Brauchitsch's reluctance to engage in a possible full-scale European war at this time, he could give –

and indeed had given – the order to crush Czecho-Slovakia in less than three weeks' time. In a few days he was to have the unsought glory of the pleading visit of the obsequious British Prime Minister Neville Chamberlain. ('It was such a bonus to his vanity,' said one of his secretaries, 'that he could scarcely contain himself with glee.') But for the moment the rally was enough. For eight days he had proved himself master of Europe. Even the London *Times*, which he believed to be the voice of the British government, had suggested appeasing him by surrendering the Sudetenland. He no doubt felt that the humiliation he had suffered in May had been avenged. Greater Germany indeed. And greater and greater Hitler.

On the following day, Tuesday 13th September, the great exodus from Nuremberg began. The machinery of the organization moved as precisely in clearing the town as it did in filling it. The hundreds of special trains took away the thousands of delegates, Party members, helpers and officials. Convoys of lorries transported the Hitler Youth, the Labour Corps, the athletes, the women, the musicians, technicians and constructional workmen. The mobile army units went away in their vehicles and the infantry marched. The tents were struck, the field kitchens and canteens dismantled, the thousands of banners lowered, the documentation begun.

Each of the eight days of the rally had had its separate theme: Welcome, Congress, Labour, Fellowship, Politics, Youth, the Storm Troopers, and the Army. There had been marches, presentations, parades by daylight and torchlight, reviews, games, meetings, exhibitions, inspections, speeches. A million people had been involved and £1,000,000 had been spent (about £3,000,000 by today's figuring). The organization had been a triumph for the ruffianly Dr Robert Ley, one of Hitler's closest confidants. His final touch was to have a hoarding built on to a triumphal arch erected across the main exit from the town. 'Goodbye until 1939', it read.

Thus ended the last and greatest of the Nazi rallies.

Menace

The first and smallest of the Nazi rallies was held in Munich at the end of January 1923. It had no declared theme. But in retrospect it is easy to attach one to it: Menace.

Though small in comparison with the later huge gatherings at Nuremberg, it was by no means ill attended. The official Party records claim 20,000 'spectators and Party members' and that is by no means improbable. Hitler had proved himself very capable not only at organizing but at impressing political assemblies. He had been in charge of the organization and propaganda of the National Socialist German Labour Party (i.e. the *National-*

sozialistische Deutsche Arbeiterpartei, abbreviated to 'Nazi') since 1920 and had raised the attendances from 111, when he addressed the Party for the first time in October 1919, to nearly 2,000 at the first meeting that he personally organized in February 1920. His ability to do this was based on two qualities.

First, he recognized, however reluctantly, that he had no power to convince individuals. Against an intellectual combatant he was incapable of rational argument because his intellect was inferior and could grasp only the most dog-eared notions. Met by argument as to the lack of originality in his political principles he could resort only to abuse. He could have been trounced in polemics by the most third-rate mind, his own being at best tenth-rate. Knowing this may well have proved unpalatable; but he had the cunning to turn the knowledge to account instead of brooding on it.

Turning aside as if in contempt, then, from the controversialist who could have torn the straw and rags of his pan-Germanic clichés to shreds in a trice, he looked to the opposite extreme – the listening, agog,

The first and smallest rally

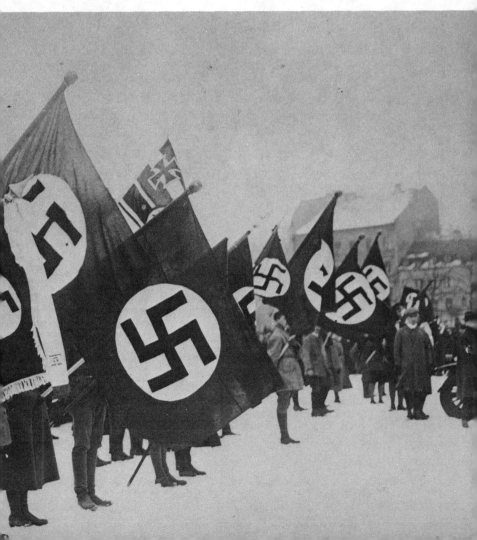

emotional crowd. His ego was satisfied in this jump from one extreme to the other by the simple and obviously true statement made in *Mein Kampf*, 'The broad masses of a nation are not made up of professors and diplomats'. Indeed they are not. They are made up of people who he describes as if he were doing a self-portrait:

'The receptive powers of the masses are very limited, and their understanding is feeble. On the other hand, they quickly forget. Such being the case, all effective propaganda must be confined to a few bare essentials and these must be expressed as far as possible in stereotyped formulas. These slogans should be persistently repeated until the very last individual has come to grasp the idea that has been put forward.' (Just as everyone knows that Guinness Is Good For You.) 'If this principle be forgotten and if an attempt be made to be abstract and generalise, the propaganda will turn out ineffective; for the public will not be able to digest or retain what is offered to them in this way. Therefore, the greater the scope of the message that has to be presented, the more necessary it is for the propaganda to discover that plan of action which is psychologically the most efficient.'

Here, then, was Hitler addressing himself to the task of implanting his chauvinistic ideas into the minds of thousands rather than individuals – seemingly, perhaps, a daunting task but in fact a much simpler one, for he could aim, so to speak, at the lowest common denominator: himself.

Secondly, Hitler was always able to hit upon 'the plan of action which is psychologically the most efficient'. And the plan of action was always based on the principle that truth must invariably be 'adjusted'.

'What should we say of a poster which purported to advertise some new brand of soap by insisting on the excellent qualities of the competitive brands? We should naturally shake

The embryo dictator : Munich 1923

our heads. And it ought to be just the same in a similar kind of political advertisement. The aim of Propaganda is not to try to pass judgement on conflicting rights, giving each its due, but exclusively to emphasize the right which we are asserting. Propaganda must not investigate the truth objectively, and, in so far as it is favourable to the other side, present it according to the theoretical rules of justice; but it must present only that aspect of the truth which is favourable to its own side.'

From the basic principle of the violation of objective truth whenever it suited the Party's book, Hitler moved on to scheme the actual methods of capturing the masses' attention so that they could be assembled and harangued.

In the earliest days, when the Party had only seven members who met weekly and in their committee meetings went round and round in the ever-decreasing circles of parish-pump politics, there was no publicity at all. Hitler took that in hand at once. There was no money either (the Party's funds totalled 7.50 marks), but clearly it was necessary to interest the public, otherwise the Party would remain at seven members for ever.

'We decided to hold a monthly meeting to which the public should be invited. Some of the invitations were typewritten, and some were written by hand. For the first few meetings we distributed them in the streets and delivered them personally at certain houses. Each one canvassed among his own acquaintances and tried to persuade some of them to attend our meetings. The result was lamentable.'

Only the same old seven members turned up, whereupon one of the first principles of advertising struck Hitler: that in choosing acquaintances to advertise to he was preaching to the converted – converted either to boredom with the Party's notions or to an agreement with them that was too limp to be useful. Any advertising is directly successful only with a pro-

Above: The embryo followers: Munich 1923. *Left:* Felix Allfarth, killed in the November 1923 putsch

portion of those it reaches; but as the audience reached becomes greater so, naturally, does the number with which it is successful.

The next step, then, was to widen the distribution of invitations; and as the cost of printing was beyond the Party's funds, Hitler duplicated by hectograph the notices advertising the next meeting. It was a little more successful and those who attended were browbeaten into contributing to the Party funds. Thus, after a couple more meetings Hitler was able to reach a still wider audience by taking space in the Munich *Beobachter*.

This time a relatively great success was achieved. The Munich Hofbräu-haus Keller was almost filled – with the 111 people who formed Hitler's first audience. From then on there was a steady increase in the attendances – and an equally steady increase in Hitler's ability to handle them. His method then and always was to work himself up into an emotional lather that, so to speak, brushed off on to his audience. In no circumstances would he – nor could he – appeal to the mind. Wherever he could he chose words that were the unmistakable coinage of brutality – and the simplest words possible. 'Hate,' 'smash,' 'kill,' force,' 'lash,' 'kick,' were all favourites. The choice of them accorded with his view that everything must be presented in black and white, no intermediate shades ever being allowed to creep in.

The magic power of the spoken word: that was what Hitler believed in. His audiences too. And indeed, if vehemence and fanaticism drive the sledgehammer that beats the words into the numbed minds of the listeners there is little to quarrel with in that view. (The effectiveness of the written word he denied – for the obvious reason that it allows for contemplation.) A ranting fanatic will rarely fail to put over ideas, however muddled and dotty they are, if he lops every qualification from them, never conceding an inch to an opposing or moderating view, and smashes the words into his audience as if they expressed the only truth that has ever been revealed.

The ideas that he presented were of course by no means new. They all stemmed from the premise that the structure of a successful society must have racial purity as its foundation. The fact that there is no such thing as racial purity in Europe or anywhere else is no obstacle to forming an ideology. And of all European nations the Germans were most receptive to that ideology.

Aggressive chauvinism manifested itself in Germany in the early nineteenth century. It was built up from the hatred of the French occupation, which had resulted in the final crumbling of the German Second Empire. An earlier fanatic than Hitler, Adam Müller, stated uncompromisingly, 'Everything Great, everything Deep, everything Durable in European institutions is German.' To a nation that had suffered the indignity of conquest and occupation the statement was balm; besides which, it was a half truth. There had been much great thought and achievement in Germany. And for a people deeply humiliated a half truth is as good as a whole one. Better. It gives plenty of scope for 'adjustment'.

There was no question of a proud nation invoking pride, honour and

courage to rise from the dust beneath the conqueror's heel: the attitude was one of, in the easy phrase, 'a chip on the shoulder'; but a chip on the shoulder reinforced by a native characteristic of malleability and love of authority for its own sake. Generally speaking, Germans love letting others do their thinking for them and obeying the next up the ladder of the hierarchy. It makes life simpler.

So, presented with ideas that were balm to their self-conscious inferiority, plus a movement, a Party, that was from top to bottom the epitome of authoritarianism, they

Left: Ernst Röhm not yet in uniform
Below: 9th November 1923: barriers

could scarcely turn away. There was a place for everybody. Particularly, there was a place for the follower rather than the leader. Leaders would always declare themselves, as had Hitler. And the method of their selection was simple enough, and was stated in *Mein Kampf:*

'Every movement which has gained its human material must first divide this material into two groups: followers and members. The follower of a movement is he who understands and accepts its aims, the member is he who fights for them. The follower has been converted by propaganda to the doctrine of the movement. The member will be charged . . . to collaborate in winning over new followers from whom in turn new members can be

recruited. Because of its passive character, the simple effort of believing in a political doctrine is enough for the majority, for the majority of mankind is mentally lazy and timid. To be a member one must be intellectually active . . . so the propagandist must seek untiringly to acquire new followers for the movement, whereas the organizer or leader must diligently look for the best elements among such followers, so that these elements may be transformed into members. The propagandist need not bother too much about the personal worth of the individuals he has won for the movement. He need not enquire into their abilities, intelligence or character. From them, however, the organizer will have to select those individuals who are most capable of actively helping to bring the movement to victory.'

Hitler states and re-states these self-evident principles of Party selection through many turgid pages. Tedious tautology was his forte. He never wrote once anything that could be written six times – a literary habit he caught from his own speechmaking; though there it was more justified according to his own rule of persistently repeating everything 'until the very last individual has come to grasp the idea that has been put forward'. Truly, the less said of Hitler's writings the better; and to avoid quoting them would be better still. But they are too revealing to be ignored altogether. Had he been frustrated in all his egotistical endeavours and never attained his famous infamy, his writings would still have revealed his character as completely as his actions did.

They reveal, for one thing – if nothing else does – that his sense of humour was completely warped. It is true that most humour is to some extent based on the discomfort of others; but to him only the extremes of cruelty and humiliation were funny. *Mein Kampf* means My Struggle; but Hitler's was a *Kampf*

Above: The two faces of menace: Hitler and Streicher. *Right:* 9th November 1923: before the march

um die Macht – a Struggle for Power; and it was punctuated by bouts of maniacal laughter. It is recorded in *The Unholy City* by Joshua Podro that when *Gauleiter* Streicher told him that he had driven 250 Jews into a field and, aided by his whip, had forced them to pull up the grass with their teeth, Hitler 'laughed uncontrollably'. Such was the sort of joke he enjoyed. And such was the unendearing character who in 1920 began to propagate the polished-up notions of a faded pan-Germanism.

By 1923 Hitler had drawn to himself and the Party the attention of far more people than the 20,000 who came to the first rally. Much of that attention was drawn by force. Germany was permitted only a token army of 100,000 after the 1918 armistice – officially. But there were hundreds of ex-servicemen who had been formed into a volunteer force – the *Freikorps* – and it was this force from which was taken the nucleus of the Storm Troops, the Nazi private army. It was called by the official euphemism 'Gymnastic and Sports Division' to avoid being disbanded by the Allies. But its purpose as declared in the Party Proclamation dated 3rd August 1921 was far from gymnastic or sporting. It was in fact, 'to serve as a means for bringing our youthful members together in a powerful organization for the purpose of utilizing their strength as an offensive force at the disposal of the movement'.

There was a vague pretence that their purpose at political meetings was to throw out anyone who attempted to break up the proceedings; but in fact they were used almost entirely as provocators, disturbers of the peace, and beaters-up of meetings of opposing political factions. Hitler bawled at a meeting in Munich on 4th January 1921:

'The National Socialist Movement in Munich will in future ruthlessly prevent – if necessary by force– all meetings or lectures that are likely to distract the minds of our fellow countrymen.'

The statement was blatant enough, and the voice correspondingly harsh. There was, however, considerable subtlety in the action it proposed. A display, or threat, of physical force is not necessarily repellent to all people: to some, violence has a strong psychological attraction – it certainly had to a great many of the post-war Germans nursing their hatreds. To them also, the feeling of being associated with a movement that was surging forward with irresistible power was like an injection of the same power into their veins. But besides both those regrettably appealing qualities there was also the propaganda value of terrorism. In pursuing its aims it is bound to attract attention, whether favourable or not.

Hitler did not personally have to soil his hands with the blood drawn by his strong-arm thugs, though there was plenty of evidence to suggest he

would have been willing enough to do so if necessary. He had, to direct the activities of the Storm Troops, one Ernst Röhm, a brutal, bitter, homosexual army officer who was one of the original members of the Party; and Hermann Göring, the air ace whose career in the war had proved him fearless, but who nourished inside his gross clown's body a ruthless, corrupt bully seeking an outlet like the evil genie in a glittering lamp. These two did all the dirty work that was necessary – Röhm forming a convenient link with the military authorities, such as they were; and Göring having the actual command of the thugs. They could hardly have been bettered for their ability to put into effect the words Hitler used when addressing a meeting in Munich in November 1922:

'Our motto shall be "If you will not be a German, I will bash your skull in". For we are convinced that we cannot succeed without a struggle. We have to fight with ideas, but, if necessary, also with our fists.'

It was scarcely surprising that with so much thuggery in support Hitler was easily 'attracting' followers. But besides the element of physical force all the theatrical trappings of melodrama were present – a symbol, a gesture of reverence, a password, a uniform. In fact all the reach-me-down appeals to those who want to 'belong'. 'Togetherness' is a word – or rather, a non-word – coined as a slogan by a women's magazine in much more recent days; but it fairly describes the superficial, sentimental urge of the German nation toward unity in the early 1920s. The Versailles Treaty had cast them down and dismembered them, and visual manifestations that the crushed body would not lie down were essential.

The symbol, the swastika, was already there – had been in existence for centuries. There was no particularly sinister significance in it – in ancient civilizations it was, if anything, a charm against the evil eye.

But it was bold, and had been used by an earlier version of the Nazi party formed before the war. Hitler brought it to prominence by using it on the Party's flag – and using it in the way that gave it its most striking impact. He knew something of colour and design, having in his early days of scratching for a living in Vienna painted posters for shopkeepers (one of them advertised Teddy Perspiration Powder), and he worked out many versions of the flag before deciding on the one that had the swastika in a white circle on a red ground.

The salute with the rigidly upflung arm was a reverential gesture to aggression rather than to peace, which is the normal meaning of a

salute. And the phrase *Sieg Heil!* ('To Victory') became not only the greeting and farewell of the Party followers but a chant to be reiterated endlessly on all public occasions.

All these melodramatic trappings helped to make and secure the lifeline that held Hitler to his public. It was an audience of adherents far greater in number than the 20,000 who gathered in Munich on 26th January 1923. The 20,000 were merely the available nucleus who had been able to reach the town where their demagogic Messiah was preaching and whose sermon would be reported throughout Germany. All the same, though rapidly snowballing in numbers they were limited geographically to

9th November 1923: the marchers start off

Bavaria; and it was to enlarge the movement to national proportions that Hitler called the first of the *Parteitage* or rallies.

The Bavarian government, having had considerable experience of the rioting and bloodshed that attended Hitler's assemblies, banned the meeting and the chief of police, a man named Nortz, was adamant against Hitler's pleas to raise the ban. Hitler could be a Uriah Heep when occasion demanded, and he went cap in hand. But his obsequiousness turned to fury at Nortz's refusal, and he threatened that his Storm Troops would make open warfare in the streets if the police or the army opened fire.

The outcome of that threat was a lifting of the ban. It was brought about by the machinations of Röhm, who with cunning duplicity convinced the government that the army would open fire on the Party demonstration if necessary. He was thus playing the army in which he held a commission against the Storm Troops which he had helped to form.

Although the *Bayrischer Kurier* reported that 'In the last few days Munich has become the scene of an ugly party battlefield', there were in fact very few incidents involving violence. The railway refused to run a special train from Stuttgart to Munich, and a few Party members were arrested by local police at Gera for disorderly conduct and later released. In general, though, the thousands arrived and were quartered without any noteworthy strife.

The programme at this and the next rally followed a different pattern from that which was evolved for the later ones. The chief difference was that in 1923 Hitler spoke at every meeting, at the most dramatically effective time – the end. In the rallies to come he was to restrict his speeches to those for which the world held its breath. But now his concern was with Germany's political future. And, of course, his own. Every possible opportunity to impress his personality on the multi-

tudes must be seized, every possible angle of attack on the ruling power covered.

The ruling order at the time was the hated Weimar republic, constituted to uphold the provisions of the Versailles Treaty. But as a national government ostensibly governing from Berlin its powers were weakened by the continued existence of independent governments in the States of Prussia, Saxony, Würtemberg . . . and Bavaria. These regional governments had the power to veto any rulings issued from Berlin. It was this unstable situation that prevailed as Hitler took the stage at the Munich rally.

At the reception in the *Fürstensalon* on the first day Hitler welcomed delegates from what the *Völkischer Beobachter* called 'far and wide'. The *Beobachter* was a Nazi-owned newspaper and said what it was told to say. But in fact the reception proved that the Party had attracted many delegates from farther afield than southern Germany. And Hitler emphasised the importance of the spreading net of Nazism:

'There are Party members here from Prague and Salzburg who will tell you of the beastly conditions in which citizens of those German territories live like slaves and of their willingness to fight for Great

Armed Nazis, March 1923

Röhm, uniformed now, stands on Hitler's left, Ludendorff on Hitler's right

Germany against the enemies of the Party.'

Clearly even in those early days territorial expansion was part of the Nazi programme. 'Greater Germany', though not the main theme of the rally as it was in 1938, was certainly one of the subsidiary ones.

The main attacks of all the speakers were against the Weimar republic, the Versailles Treaty, reparations, the monetary system, the presence of French troops in the Ruhr valley, and the 'November criminals' – Hitler's

effective term for those who had been instrumental in bringing about the surrender of 11th November 1918. Diatribe after diatribe pushed home these attacks. Frenzied unanimity was gained on all points. Hitler was unanimously elected chairman of the new executive committee. The treasurer reported that contributions to Party funds now totalled 'millions' (of marks presumably). Dietrich Eckart, editor of the *Völkischer Beobachter*, was personally thanked by Hitler for having publicized the movement 'in the spirit of accurate and truthful journalism, telling the

nation the whole truth of the disasters that would overwhelm the country until the Nazis were completely in power'. And as a *bonne bouche* for Eckart the announcement was made that as from the next issue the paper would be published daily instead of weekly.

On the third day all the resolutions that had been passed at the opening meeting were passed again in different words. The rally was a rally of words, words, words. With one exception ceremony and spectacle had not yet become established. Hitler was too concerned to establish himself. And

establish himself he did – as also, by way of the wide publicity gained by the rally, the pan-German ideas of Nazism. If the world did not now know of the Nazi hatreds – Judaism, Marxism, pacifism, the French, the instigators of Versailles and 'the November criminals' – and the Nazi objectives – the ruthless overthrow of the Weimar republic and the acquisition of territories adjoining Germany – it was no fault of Hitler and his minions. 'Herr Hitler,' the *Morning Post* reported, raising its eyebrows in a well-bred British way, 'appears to be a forceful and ambitious man.'

43

Success and rebellion

The single example of ceremony that gave the Munich rally such spectacle as it had was the Consecration of the Flags. This rite was performed then and at every subsequent rally, though for the time being it was far from impressive and had not acquired the solemn, *quasi* religious grandeur that would belong to it after the events of the following November.

The ceremony was held in a large open space, the Märzfeld. It was bitterly cold and flurries of snow whirled down on the thousands of spectators. They watched the Storm

Troopers arrive – 5,000 of them according to the *Völkischer Beobachter* – and take up their places on the parade ground. They were carefully drilled but had no weapons or uniforms; there was, however, a certain uniformity about the Tyrolean hats, short overcoats, and thick stockings with trousers tucked into them that the majority wore. And of course they carried the Nazi banners – one to each group of a hundred.

The emotional effect of music had not, even at that first rally, been forgotten. A local band played a traditional thanksgiving song *Niederländisches Dankgebet* and all stood with bared heads. The *Beobachter* notes the 'unifying effect' of the singing – hardly a masterly stroke of deduction. At the end of the song there was a short silence, then Hitler addressed the multitude – presumably without the aid of any public address equipment, since these were early days for microphones and loudspeakers and the available pictures show no

Greetings from Ludendorff for a provincial contingent of Nazis, 1924

megaphone. Hitler stands bare-headed in the snow like a waif in a storm, except for the long-handled whip that hangs from his belt – hardly a waif-like accoutrement. Heinrich Hoffmann, who joined the Party about the same time as Hitler, and from then on remained the only man allowed to photograph him, has taken the picture from a low angle to give Hitler height; but he hasn't succeeded in making him impressive.

The address was concerned with the symbolism of the flag. The red, Hitler said, represented the blood of the Party, the white was for national strength and purity, and the swastika would remind everyone of the struggle for victory of Aryan man over the forces of Jewry and Marxism. That gave him a lead-in to a solemn declaration that no Jew or Marxist would ever be allowed to soil the flag by touching it. He then called upon the Storm Troopers to vow that they would never abandon the banner in any circumstances except death.

Whether or not there was any means of amplifying Hitler's voice the audience seems to have got the message. There were 'tumultuous cries of support and thousands swore there and then to follow the movement'. So says the *Beobachter* – a somewhat prejudiced source of information admittedly. But a captive audience disposed to accept the platitudes of pan-Germanism and presumably mesmerized by Hitler's melodramatic style and tub-thumping gestures (Arnold Toynbee notes in *Acquaintances* that he had beautiful hands and used a wealth of gesture) were no doubt ready to rally to the flag and the Party.

Immediately after the flag ceremony the Storm Troopers marched past Hitler with banners lowered. It took three quarters of an hour for the five thousand to pass the saluting base and for all that time Hitler stood with his arm in the uncomfortable Nazi salute. As the Märzfeld cleared the snow began to fall more heavily.

In the evening there was a packed audience at the Hofbrauhaus for more political speeches and another rally tradition was started: the playing of an overture as Hitler entered. The orchestra was the Munich Symphony Orchestra and the overture was Wagner's *Rienzi*. The playing of it gained Hitler the reputation of being intensely musical, which he was not. He acted a dutiful devotion to Wagner, enjoyed light operas such as The Merry Widow, and was stimulated by the more dramatic overtures and symphonies of Beethoven and Brahms. But beyond that he did not go – though naturally he convinced himself along with everybody else that he was as authoritative and appreciative toward music as he was toward art and architecture. His real purpose in having Wagner played in the Hofbräuhaus that night was to pander to the artists and intellectuals who might be persuaded to join the Party. 'They can be useful,' he told Streicher 'One must have a leavening of intellectuals, for they disperse ideas in a different way.' Besides, the playing of dramatic music during his entry was satisfying to his megalomania; and he evidently noted the effect, for every future rally had the same feature.

It was on this occasion too that he arrived at the sound psychological conclusion that the most important speeches should always be made in the evening. 'At eight o'clock at night,' he wrote, 'man's resistance is at its lowest. His strenuous day's work is over and his mind is receptive – even to lies.'

On the subject of lies he was, as it were, extremely truthful so far as his own were concerned:

'In the big lie there is always a certain force of credibility; because the broad masses of a nation are always more easily corrupted in the deeper strata of their emotional nature than consciously or voluntarily, and thus in the primitive

Stresemann, the Chancellor

46

simplicity of their minds they more readily fall victims to the big lie than the small lie, since they themselves often tell small lies in little matters but would be ashamed to resort to large-scale falsehoods. It would never come into their heads to fabricate colossal untruths, and they would not believe that others could have the impudence to distort the truth so infamously. Even though the facts which prove this to be so may be brought clearly to their minds, they will still doubt and waver and still continue to think that there may be some other explanation.'

The broad masses listening to him at the Munich rally were not treated to any of the wilder of Hitler's lies. The time had not yet come for those. What they heard was the dogmatic reiteration of the basic tenets of the Nazi Party. Speaker after speaker pounded away at Versailles, the 'November criminals', the combined threats of Judaism and Marxism, the Weimar republic, the betrayal of the German soldiers who had fought for their country, the importance of 'blood purity', the great German traditions, the theft of her empire by inferior nations; and of course the implied promise of leadership in a revolt against the forces of evil.

The revolt – the *putsch* – was to come later that year. But preceding it was the second of the rallies. And this time, at the instance of Julius Streicher, who had made his sacrificial gesture by allowing his splinter-group party to be absorbed by the Nazis, the venue was changed to Nuremberg.

At that time, 1923, Streicher was a school teacher there, a bulky, arrogant man with a big nose, small eyes, projecting ears, and a spherical shaven head. He was a model for the savage satire of the artist Georg Grosz, who drew him again and again in bitter delineations of German militarism and corruption. Seventeen years later even Hitler was to have him arrested and thrown out of the

Party for corrupt use of official funds; but for the moment he was a swaggering pervert in the right place at the right time to be of use to Hitler.

Nuremberg, Streicher pointed out, was the ideal focal point for Party activities – a far from unjust claim.

The town's history from the Dark Ages onward is riddled with the elements of chauvinism. Goths, Germans, Franks and Huns defended its fortress against Slav attacks and its commerce against Jewish infiltrations. Attila, Charlemagne and Barbarossa either plundered or were welcomed into the town and touched its traditions with the glamour of their names. Bavarian nobles and Hohenstaufen kaisers dignified the place with charters and courts. At least one saint – St Sebald – was enshrined there for his miracles, his shrine overlooking the market place where on St Nicholas' eve in 1298 all the 307 Jews in the town were bound tightly together with chains and burned alive. Clearly Nuremberg had the highest historical credentials as a German town.

Geographically also it was near the ideal, though the scenery is not specially rewarding. (Longfellow in his poem about the town could squeeze no more than two lines' worth out of the possibilities: 'In the valley of the Pegnitz, where across broad meadow lands/Rise the blue Franconian mountains, Nuremberg the ancient stands.') But scenery was not a necessary quality for a Nazi congress centre. Far more important were the facts that it is much nearer the centre of Germany, that seven railway lines converge there (the *Ludwigsbahn* between Nuremberg and Fürth was the first German railway to be opened, in 1835) and that there are adequate roads and waterways.

Architecturally it was of course famous for its Gothic, its moat, its castle, and its Rathaus (town hall) complete with medieval torture chamber. Even that grim dungeon harboured a uniquely famous con-

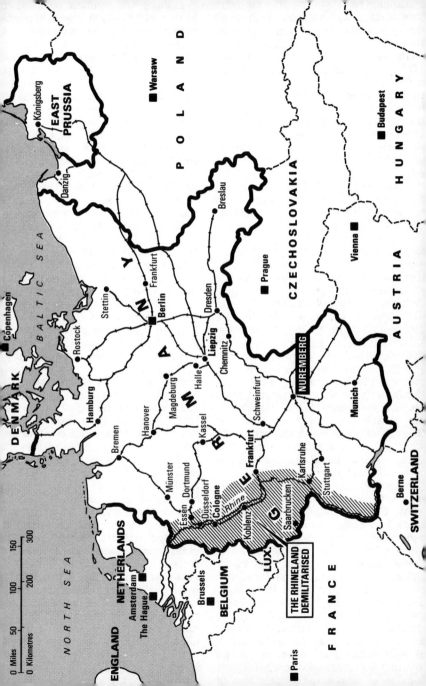

trivance, the 'Nuremberg Maiden'. The Maiden was an iron mechanical figure crudely resembling a woman. Ingenious machinery enabled it to clasp its victim in a spiked grip, the spikes being placed to pierce his eyes, navel, genitals and anus. The robot then released him and dropped his body on to a series of revolving disc knives which sliced him to pieces. The apparatus was a special object of reverence for Streicher, who prowled about the dungeon frequently, like a pilgrim at worship.

There were of course more appealing Nurembergian crafts and arts than the torturing of racial and heretic victims. The first paper mill in Europe was set up there in 1370. The clarinet, the airgun and the wire-drawing machine were invented there. The first practical watch was made there in 1500, its shape dictating that from that day to this it should be known as the 'Nuremberg Egg'. (It was made by an horologist named Peter Henlein, from whom Konrad Henlein, Hitler's viceroy in the Sudetenland, claimed an improbable direct descent.) The first printed playing cards came from Nuremberg. Brass in its present form was invented there by Erasmus Ebner, and military cannon were first cast there. And of course it was the birthplace of Albrecht Dürer and Hans Sachs. One way and another Nuremberg had much to commend it.

It is evident that the idea of a second rally could not have been far from Hitler's mind. The Munich affair had been successful in that it had exacerbated the despair felt by the German nation for the weakness of the Weimar government. The Party had gained thousands of declared new members and, even more important, had achieved the national publicity that infiltrated its policy through to thousands more potential followers. And Hitler had in all he said revealed himself as the ruthless enemy of the reparations that accounted for the country's economic depression, of military inferiority, and of disunity.

Though the Munich occasion had been a rally only in the rudimentary sense it had revealed a glimpse of the scope of such Party congresses. To a demagogue like Hitler there must have seemed limitless possibilities. His lust for personal power would have overridden any realization that his actual achievements to date were merely those of a provincial windbag, rustling – though somewhat disturbingly – the dusty answers of the fraily established politicians. Impressed by Streicher's notions regarding Nuremberg he decided to reinforce success with a second rally; and this time a more carefully organized one.

An historical excuse lay readily to hand. In September 1870 Prussian troops had received Napoleon III's surrender at the battle of Sedan. 'That great German victory,' said Hitler, 'will be the theme of our congress.'

In the event little attention was given to the great German victory. Historic occasions earlier than the First World War had little practical significance for the Nazis. A token exhibition with a few documents and a model showing the strategical disposition of the opposing troops at the battle was displayed in the Luitpold hall; but that was about all. For the rest the emphasis was very heavily on the present and future.

There was also a great deal more planning. Julius Streicher and Willy Liebel, who was at that time only a member of the town council, together organized everything. They had some hold over the mayor, Dr Luppe, who was sympathetic toward the Communist movement in the town, and forced his co-operation – without, apparently, much opposition from the main body of the citizenry, who at Luppe's behest had reluctantly beflagged and beflowered their houses in honour of a Communist youth rally held in May. They were far more willingly prepared to give a welcome to the Nazis, of whose manifesto, published on the eve of the rally, they heartily approved.

'The congress,' the manifesto said, 'shall be our way of demonstrating our will and desire to change Nuremberg and make it again the centre of national unity and defence, just as it used to be.'

It continued militantly about the Nazi aims: 'Peace and quiet are not political ideas worth fighting for. Quite often peace and quiet are nothing more than laziness and mental atrophy. Not one nation has ever been saved with peace and quiet. On the contrary, nations have been destroyed and defeated through it. Peace is of importance only when it shelters the adventurous life, not the November criminals and the Jewish democrats on the stock exchange . . . But the people of Nuremberg should realize finally that enthusiasm, militarism, and organizations as such are of no importance in the struggle for freedom unless they are fighting for a clearly defined German goal. We must stop the illusion that somewhere in our country today there exists a local government that is worth protecting, even with one man.'

The idea that their town should be made the heart of a movement for national unity and the overthrow of the hated Weimar republic appealed strongly to the innate pan-Germanism of the Nurembergers. They saw themselves as citizens of the true German town in which medieval glories decorated the battlefield of true German ideology. They leapt to implement Streicher's ideas. Arrangements were made for the great medieval castle to be illuminated; a central bureau was established to arrange accommodation for the influx of visitors; the railway authorities were prevailed upon – or perhaps coerced – to provide special trains to bring Party members and delegates from the far more widely spread towns that now formed part of the Nazi network; and all houses and shops were to be decorated during the rally. (Refusal to do so, the public notices hinted darkly, would result in

'names of the sympathizers with international Jewry and Marxism being listed for the denial of future privileges'.) Also, Streicher cunningly arranged for companies of Storm Troopers to 'assist the police in keeping law and order', thus giving them an offiical status that could be useful in quelling, with the approved Nazi strongarm methods, any opposition that cropped up. And this time there was to be some.

At dusk on the 31st August the floodlighting was turned on and the castle was seen as it had never been seen before. 'It was a breathtaking spectacle,' wrote an English tourist who happened to be in the town at the time. Had he stayed for the rally his independent comments might have been useful; unfortunately he left early next morning on his walking tour and his article, published in *Chamber's Journal*, is concerned only with his tour. But he notes that 'this feudal town with immense fortified walls surrounded by a moat, and with the glowing night sky pierced by spires, towers and tall gables, is like a realization of one of the Grimm fairy tales. And with the great fortress standing alone on its eminence and bathed in light there is much inspiration for the imagination to wander among stories of warriors bold, fiery monsters and imprisoned maidens'.

The inspiration affected the imagination of Streicher and Liebel rather differently. On 1st September Streicher stood on the platform of the Ausstellungshalle, legs astride, hands on hips, his riding crop thrust into his jackboot, and welcomed the Party delegates from other towns. They had all arrived the day before and been marched to their quarters by squads of Storm Troopers – an experience they clearly had enjoyed for the sake of the militarism involved, which was typified by the goose-step march adopted by many of the groups, particularly those from the zones of occupied Austria and northern Germany.

Above: Streicher. *Right:* Liebel

Streicher said he welcomed them in the name of Adolf Hitler – 'who will be with us to receive the honoured guests tomorrow' – then called for an interval during which police would check the passes of everyone in the hall to make sure that 'no Jewish swine managed to evade the stringent precautions'. At this there were some voices of protest in several parts of the hall. The name of Rindfleisch was invoked. (Rindfleisch was the 13th-century fanatic who ordered the burning of the Nuremberg Jews on St Nicholas' Eve in 1298.) Streicher drew the whip from his jackboot and 'whirled it round his head like a demented ringmaster', the correspondent of *Frankischer Kurier* noted, 'while the so-called Gymnasts scuffled with Communists who had hoped to break up the meeting and ejected them, aided by the police'.

After this demonstration of welcome Streicher continued his speech, which was now concerned with the disgusting nature of the Jews' ancient crimes (mainly the crime of living), and the contrastingly glowing history of the Party in Nuremberg as built up by himself. He continued his ringmaster gestures during the speech and included many luridly descriptive passages about the rape of pure German maidens by hideously diseased and malformed Jews. (He was attempting in verbal form the pornography for which his illustrated magazine *Der Stürmer* was later to become notorious.) Had Hitler been present he would have approved of the effect created by his creature.

Hitler arrived early next morning accompanied by General Erich von Ludendorff, the revered military dictator of wartime Germany, who at that time was going through one of his crazy phases of atheism tortuously mingled with German mythology, and was revealing himself to be – though it's hardly the word – a godsend to the Nazi Party, since he still had a wide popular following as one of Germany's most brilliant military strategists. Hitler and Ludendorff then drove off

in an open touring car to the Deutsch-herrenfeld where, somewhat surprisingly, a religious service was being held – ostensibly as a memorial to the dead of the war but in fact to give Streicher and a Nuremberg parson named Schmidt an opportunity of preaching anti-Jewish doctrine from a pulpit. Presumably the pulpit and the parson's cassock added the imprimatur of the Church to peculiarly malevolent utterances.

After the service Hitler welcomed the 'guests of honour', who included a minor prince (Ludwig Ferdinand), several generals, and Admiral von Scheer of Jutland fame. This time there was no hint of the solitary waif-like Hitler addressing an uncertain rabble. Flanked at the saluting base by uniformed and influential figures he watched the great parade that Streicher and Liebel had organized as the spectacular centre of the rally.

The march-past was led by a band and a company of mounted police, followed by the crack regiment of mounted Uhlans in their colourful uniforms with their lances glinting. Behind these came marching groups of young men wearing the traditional costumes of Bavaria, the Tyrol, and other regions whose support had been gained. 'The establishment' of police, army and costumed civilians leading the parade shed upon it a most respectable radiance. The Storm Troopers, goose-stepping eight abreast behind, were so to speak the tail of the comet. It was an astute move on Streicher's part to imply by the order of march that the Storm Troopers had the approval of officialdom; and to have a troop of cavalry bringing up the rear of the Storm Troopers – who this time were described as 'industrial workers' and were uniformly dressed in brown shirts with swastika armbands – added a final emphasis.

In all, 80,000 men marched past the saluting base and their parade lasted two hours. It was followed by the ceremony of the consecration of the flags, at which Pastor Schmidt officiated with Hitler. Hitler, a Roman Catholic by upbringing but long lapsed as a member of the Church, had taken care to appease the atheistic Ludendorff by reminding him that 'military objectives are often achieved by devious routes'. Ludendorff says in his memoirs that he was 'astonished by this embracing of the Church' but was 'convinced of its efficacy' when Hitler referred to the events of the rally as 'the memorable success of German Day 1923', after which the General conceded that any methods were justified in achieving the overthrow of the Berlin government including the blessing of the Nazi flag 'with so-called holy water'

It was partly in consequence of Ludendorff's reference that day to the overthrow of the Berlin government (Weimar was the town where the 1919 constitution had been worked out, but the seat of government was of course Berlin) that Hitler decided on his next move. The idea of leading a revolt had been uppermost in his mind since he had breathed life into the moribund Party with its seven members endlessly discussing the fruitless agendas of routine committee meetings. But he was feeling his way. Throughout his career his ability to seize the psychological moment for action is marked. During the month of August just ended crisis after crisis had mounted in Germany: strikes and riots exacerbated by Communist agitation, intense inflation, and starvation had brought the Chancellorship of Herr Cuno toppling and his replacement by Gustav Stresemann. The French occupation of the Ruhr industrial area with the object of seizing products that had not been forthcoming under the 'agreed' reparations had resulted in a campaign of passive resistance. And the entire political and economic course of the country was headed toward disaster.

Ludendorff's bitter approval of anything – even the symbol of the Christianity he hated and attacked as vehemently as Hitler attacked Judaism – if it would bring the Wiemar republic to destruction, 'was like a spark igniting a train of events'. So Hitler said in a speech in Vienna in 1935. He had Ludendorff on his side. The country was on the verge of civil war. He would strike, make his bid for power.

But for the moment he could enjoy, and analyze, the terrific impact the first of the Nuremberg rallies was making. In every way it was overshadowing the tentative success of the January affair at Munich. Streicher and Liebel had done their job of organization superbly.

Further successes followed in the evening. The Ausstellungshalle was filled with 2,000 people who were replaced again and again by 2,000 others until Hitler had made the same speech four times. These 8,000 eager listeners cheered him enthusiastically, though he was several times interrupted by hecklers with megaphones who were seized and beaten up with truncheons by police and Storm Troopers. ('The Jewish and Marxist elements were quickly put under control,' was the *Beobachter's* description of the quelling of the disturbers.) And when next day the great march of newly consecrated banners made its way to the station there were huge cheering crowds to see them go. In isolated instances one or two attacks were made on flag bearers and the army officers escorting them, but these ill-organized incidents 'were no more than typical of the unrest that permeates the whole nation and will continue to do so until power has been gained by a strong man leading a strong party that will vanquish the system of majority rule, rebuild the nation's economy on the ruins of international capitalism, and insist that every citizen has an obligation to Germany'.

As the rally ended the strong man of the Nazi party calculated that the moment to strike had come.

Suppression and survival

The political situation worsened in the weeks following the first Nuremberg rally. That is, from Hitler's point of view it grew better because it was a situation of many conflicting elements and instability is a prerequisite of revolution.

In Berlin Stresemann's government agreed to continue reparations payments to France and Hitler in a speech at Munich referred bitterly to the Chancellor's ' subserviency toward the enemy, surrender of the human dignity of the German, pacifist cowardice, tolerance of every indig-nity, readiness to agree to everything until nothing remains'. In Saxony the regional government was threatened by a revolutionary element of Communists almost as powerful as were the Nazis in Bavaria, and there were equally strong Communist revolutionary organizations in the industrial areas of the Ruhr and Hamburg. In the Rhineland there were Separatists, and in the north there was a segment of the regular army called the *Schwarz Reichswehr* (Black Army) which had

9th November 1923

Above: **Marching through Weimar**
Right: **Hitler's arrival at the Weimar rally**

been organized secretly to evade the restrictions of the Versailles Treaty and which already under its leader Major Buchrucker, was planning to revolt. Stresemann's government certainly had its hands full.

It could look only to the army to control the situation. The Commander-in-Chief, General Hans von Seeckt, was not against Hitler (he was later to join the Party), but he was violently against the Left. Stresemann, helpless at the head of the crumbling republic, could only wonder if the High Command would come down on the side of the Nazis and usurp constitutional authority. But in fact Seeckt was too far-seeing a leader to undermine the constitution and cause a flare-up that would undoubtedly lead to civil war if he supported the Nazis even though he sympathized with many of their

aims. He issued an Order of the Day that was to become famous in German history. It was dated 4th November 1923 and read, in part:

'As long as I am in Command I shall continue to repeat that salvation for Germany cannot come from one extreme or the other, neither through help from abroad nor through revolution, whether of the Right or the Left. It is only by hard work, silently and persistently pursued, that we can survive. This can only be accomplished on the basis of the legal constitution. To abandon this principle is to unleash civil war. In such a civil war it would be impossible for any of the parties to win: it would be a conflict that could end only in their mutual destruction, a conflict similar to that of which the Thirty Years War provides so terrible an example.'

Seeckt's proclamation followed the government's action a week earlier, when emergency powers had been granted to the army. The High Command was now indeed in command.

Left: Von Kahr, who refused Hitler permission to hold meetings in Munich in 1924. *Right:* Von Lossow, hand in glove with Kahr against Hitler in 1923
Far right: Von Seeckt: his proclamation of 4th November 1923 became famous in German history

Any attempt by revolutionary parties to overthrow the régime by force would be met, not by unarmed police, but by the military.

However, this emergency move to gain control strong enough to deal with threatened insurrections was not in practice as powerful as it was in theory. It was weakened, of course, by the fact already mentioned – that regional governments had too autonomous a status, which enabled them to veto the rulings of Berlin. Certainly they could not veto the High Command's threat of military force on their own, since the army was far from united and Major Buchrucker's Black Army was by no means the only military revolutionary group. In Bavaria particularly the opposition was strong. The Bavarian state armed forces were commanded by General Otto von Lossow, who was hand in glove with the State Commissioner, Gustav von Kahr, a dictatorial man who hoped to restore the monarchy in Bavaria and was quite willing – indeed anxious – to do battle with Berlin in the literal sense.

Although the extreme right-wing sympathies of Kahr and Lossow may be seen as highly suitable for Hitler's rebellious scheme to flourish in, there was in fact a great deal of antipathy between them. It was caused by Kahr's refusal to allow Hitler to hold mass meetings in Munich at the end of September. It seems likely that those meetings, backed by the call-up of the entire 15,000 Storm Troopers under Göring's command and the support of Lossow's Bavarian army were intended as the initiation of the revolutionary march on Berlin and the overthrow of Stresemann's government. Their suppression by a man from whom he had every expectation of co-operation caused Hitler to go into one of his ungovernable rages.

'I thought he would collapse in a state of apoplexy,' Kahr afterward said. 'There was foam on his mouth, his speech became completely incoherent, and he kicked chairs and tables from his path as he raged up and down the Cabinet room. He smote at walls and my desk with his clenched fists until they swelled with bruised flesh. I have never seen so maniacal a performance. Raging though he was

with threats of bloody revolution it was impossible to take him seriously, and I did not give way.'

Thus Hitler's time scheme for the Nazi seizure of power had been upset by the Bavarian government's alarm at the thought of uncontrollable power springing up within its bailiwick. But the increasing confusion between the end of September and the end of October, when the state of national emergency was proclaimed and the High Command of the army took over the executive powers of government, offered him another chance. Perhaps a better one. Who could yet tell?

Hitler now saw that some merely inflammatory action would be a better deed to better the day. Still on the crest of the wave of propaganda gained by the success of the Nuremberg rally, he arranged with the editor of the *Völkischer Beobachter* to print articles about Stresemann and Seeckt that could scarcely fail to inflame relations between Berlin and Munich. Nor did they. Using all the force of a sledgehammer to crack a nut Berlin forbade the publication of the *Beobachter*. Kahr saw the ban as a mere quibble and refused to implement it; whereupon Seeckt ordered Lossow to close the paper's offices and put a guard on them. But Lossow too refused and in consequence was ordered to relinquish his command. Again Kahr defied Berlin, retorted that he as State Commissioner had commanded Lossow to remain in his post as head of the Bavarian army, and insolently demanded the immediate resignation of the Berlin government – a demand he reinforced by ordering Lossow to muster his troops.

Having thus deliberately inflamed relations between Berlin and Munich, Hitler convinced himself – and for that matter his collaborators Ludendorff, Göring and Röhm – that there would 'never be a moment when the fruit of power is riper for plucking'. Whatever

The smile on the face of the tiger

Hitler comfortably ensconsed in Landsberg

the future would prove with regard to his genius for choosing the right moments for his *coups d'etat,* his present decision was the exception – perhaps the exception that proved the rule. Hermann Rauschning says in his book *Germany's Revolution of Destruction* that Hitler's attempt at a national revolution was 'Amateurishly and sketchily improvised . . . in a whirl of romanticism; for the most part it was not the work of adults but of grown-up children'.

In fact Hitler never conceived the idea of a revolution in which his own Storm Troopers would overthrow the army of General Seeckt and take possession of the Reichstag in Berlin. Their numerical inferiority and deficiency of arms would have made that impracticable. But with the enmity between Berlin and Munich now inflamed there seemed no reason why Lossow's forces, already mustered on the borders of Bavaria and Thuringia, should not be co-opted. As Hitler said later: 'We never thought to carry through a revolt against the army: it was in collaboration with the army that we believed we should succeed'. He somewhat naïvely believed that Kahr and Lossow would have no hesitation in joining forces with him.

But he had forgotten that Kahr's Right-wing sympathies were wholeheartedly for the restoration of a monarchy in Bavaria, not for the handing over of power to an upstart dictator who had behaved like a madman in the Cabinet room only a few weeks earlier. He was reminded by the announcement that Kahr intended to hold a meeting in the Bürgerbräu Keller in Munich on the evening of 8th November. That meeting, Hitler realized now, must be intended for the proclamation of Kahr's policy of monarchic restoration.

He now had to act more quickly than he had intended. His plan had been to march into Munich on 10th November and prevail upon Kahr to join forces with him in a seizure of power. Alarmed by the thought that he would be too late he decided to act on the evening of Kahr's speech. And act he did.

According to *Der Hitler-Prozess,* the official record, the opening scene resembled nothing so much as a Western melodrama.

Having despatched one of his henchmen to fetch General Ludendorff from his home on the outskirts of the city, Hitler and Göring – they were both armed with pistols – marched at the head of a detachment of six hundred Storm Troopers to the Bürgerbräu Keller surrounded it, and put a machine gunner in the foyer. Inside, Kahr had already begun to address a large audience. Hitler and his bodyguard of armed men thrust their way past stewards into the hall. As soon as he was inside Hitler leapt on to a table piled with leaflets and fired his pistol at the ceiling. Naturally that stopped Kahr talking and caused a general sensation. The policeman on duty in the hall was as astonished as everybody else and did nothing. At once Hitler and his bodyguard marched down the centre aisle and on to the platform. Kahr was still standing with his mouth open in mid-sentence. General Lossow and Colonel Hans von Seisser, chief of the state police, who were flanking him on the platform, had made no more than a move to rise from their chairs. By the time they had risen Hitler was already on the platform and had turned to the audience:

'The national revolution has begun,' he shouted. 'This hall is surrounded by six hundred heavily armed men. No one may leave. The Bavarian and Reich governments have been deposed and a provisional national government formed. The army and police barracks have been taken over and troops and police are marching on the city under the swastika banner.'

Not a word of that was true except the statement about the armed men; but as Hitler himself had said, the bigger the lie the bigger the chance of it being accepted. In any case, no one could be sure. Armed men were clearly visible at the windows and Hitler had spoken with complete conviction. As on so many later occasions his bluff carried the day. Stunned into acceptance, the crowd watched Hitler's mien change as he ushered Kahr,

Lossow and Seisser off the platf into the adjoining green-room. 'In a short while we shall return and tell you our plans,' he said with a smile, thus giving the impression that co-operation with the others was already secure.

Such was far from the case. Lossow later said in evidence that the 'plans' amounted to Hitler pacing up and down the green-room waving his pistol and shouting that he had already formed a government with Ludendorff and that Lossow, Kahr and Seisser had better join him or he would shoot them on the spot, saving one bullet for his own suicide.

Confined to an audience of three Hitler's ranting was not so effective. It was the old problem of his inability to convince anything smaller than a mob. Lossow, Kahr and Seisser seem to have been merely bewildered. They neither agreed nor disagreed with anything Hitler said, and in a few moments he rushed to the door, pulled in one of the armed Storm Troopers and left him guarding the three astonished men before himself returning to the hall, where Göring had meanwhile been keeping order. There he once again relied on a mad bluff to achieve his aims; and mad as it was it once again succeeded.

'The government of the November criminals and the Chancellor of the Reich are declared to be removed,' he shouted. 'A new national government will be nominated this very day, here in Munich. A German national army will be formed immediately. I propose that, until accounts have finally been settled with the November criminals, the government will be headed by me. Ludendorff will take over the leadership of the German army. Lossow will be Minister for War and Seisser the Police Minister. The task of my provisional government is to organize the march on that sinful Babel, Berlin, and save the German people.'

At this there was a wild outburst of cheering, the crowd having not unreasonably assumed that Hitler

was reporting a *fait accompli*. And into the midst of the cheering crowd, as if on a precisely timed cue, Ludendorff entered.

His entry provoked more cheering, which he too naturally assumed to signify a *fait accompli*. The three men under guard in the green-room could hardly fail to be impressed by all this lustily audible enthusiasm; and when Hitler and Ludendorff joined them and Hitler's 'government' was foisted upon them it took only a few moments to bring them to the conviction that all had turned out for the best. For the time being the monstrous bluff had worked. All five now returned to the platform, made loyal speeches, swore eternal amity, and ended the meeting in an aura of backslapping breeziness reminiscent of a junior school's sports day.

It was of course inevitable that intervention must come from Berlin. It did so, very quickly. On returning to the Munich barracks Lossow and Kahr found awaiting them a telegraphed order from Seeckt to suppress the revolt or take the consequences – trial for treason. And since there was considerable lack of sympathy with Hitler's aims among some of the senior officers of the Munich garrison, a division of loyalties now made itself apparent. The schism resulted in Kahr renouncing his decision to back Hitler. 'I suddenly saw,' he said later, 'that I had been the victim of an insolent bluff.'

Having come to his senses he issued an immediate edict: the Nazi Party was to be disbanded at once, by force if necessary.

Thus it came about that on the morning of 9th November, when Hitler and Ludendorff set out from the Bürgerbräu Keller at the head of a column of some 2,000 Storm Troopers with the object of occupying the War Ministry building, they were met by a cordon of armed police.

Hitler gazes dramatically from his window in Landsberg fortress

The events of the next few minutes were confused, but the essential facts are clear. Hitler shouted 'Surrender!' to the police, there was a brief scuffle, and shots were fired by both sides. A man called Scheubner-Richter, who was marching beside Hitler and carrying the Nazi banner, fell dead. Göring too fell, wounded by a shot in the chest. And Hitler was dragged to the ground by other Nazis who were marching with him in the leading ranks and who were going down now like ninepins under a rain of bullets from police carbines.

The column was thrown into total confusion by the mowing down of the men at its head. The street was narrow, so there was no room to deploy. But there was a complete loss of nerve by everyone except Ludendorff, who marched implacably ahead and straight through the now broken cordon of police, of whom three lay dead from Nazi shots. No one had the courage to follow him. Hitler picked himself up nursing a dislocated shoulder and scuttled back to the rear of the column, where he was driven away in a waiting car that had been intended to take him to Berlin after the capture of the War Ministry building. The rest of the Storm Troopers dispersed and fled, leaving Göring to be carried into a nearby house by a couple of spectators of the sorry affair. The revolt was over, the 2,000 Storm Troopers having been broken up by rather fewer than a hundred police. Hitler was arrested two days later and charged with treason. At a twenty-four day trial he was sentenced to five years' imprisonment. Kahr's edict was upheld and the Nazi Party was proscribed throughout Germany; its funds were seized and publication of the *Völkischer Beobachter* banned.

What remained, however, was the memory of sixteen dead Nazis and a bullet-riddled banner. And nothing else has quite the survival value, in terms of propaganda, of a martyr and a blood-stained flag.

Interregnum

As a punishment, Hitler's committal to prison cannot be considered as anything but laughable. At his trial he had not made the mistake of burdening his collaborators with responsibility; and he had pleaded his own cause – the ultimate good of the Fatherland – with such rhetorical effect that the judges were far from unanimous about his guilt. The State Prosecutor won his case, however, and emphasized that the law called for a minimum of five years' imprisonment for a convicted traitor. At this there were strong protests and the presiding judge felt called upon to smooth everybody down with assurances of good treatment and early release on parole for 'so distinguished a revolutionary as Herr Hitler'. His particular kind of treason, it seemed, was a mere technicality.

Consequently, Hitler spent quite a jolly time in Landsberg Fortress and was released on parole after serving only a year of his sentence. During his 'incarceration' he was allowed full freedom of communication with the outside world. He was well fed, had a valet/secretary, and spent much of his

Marktplatz, Nuremberg 1929

time writing his turgid book which was turgidly entitled *Four and a Half Years of Struggle against Lies, Stupidity and Cowardice* – just the title for the door-stop of a book it turned out to be; though Max Amann, the publisher, presumably seeing it as one that might not spring easily to the lips of the book-buying public, shortened it to *Mein Kampf*. A pity he didn't shorten the book too. But Hitler, like all amateur writers with slovenly educations, cherished his every tedious word and went into raving tantrums at the mere suggestion of editing. The first part of his ludicrous book subscribed only seven hundred copies on publication in July 1925; but he was already mercilessly at work on Volume Two. There would come a day when *Mein Kampf* would be required reading for every German household and not to have a copy on display would incur the gravest suspicion.

Not only did Hitler live on the fat of the land while in prison – at least, such fat as was available at the time – but he also avoided the necessity of having to cope with the crazy economics that afflicted Germany in the early 1920s. Inflation had carried the price of an American dollar to four billion marks, a postage stamp to twelve billion, a newspaper to two hundred billion. Germans poured over the border into Austria, where inflation had had less effect and where one could post a letter for the Austrian equivalent of a mere million marks. The currency was stabilized by the summer of 1924 mainly as the result of the Dawes Plan, under which huge sums were lent to Germany by American investors, and the new reparations agreement with the Allies which led to the departure of occupation troops from the Ruhr and Rhineland. Stresemann's government,

Below: At the opera. *Right:* Symbolism on the stage, typifying the kind of dramatic effects that were aimed at in the rallies

The 1929 Nuremberg rally; garlanded
Nazis marching in front of the saluting
base

faithfully carrying out the constitution of the Weimar republic, gained
a complete *volte face* from a huge
majority of German citizens – not
surprisingly, since renewed vigour
had been given to German industry,
unemployment had fallen, and international relations were much
improved.

During the years 1923 to 1926 the
Party's fortunes waned far more often
than they waxed. Officially forbidden
to preach their doctrine, the Nazis
remained underground until Hitler's
release from Landsberg in December
1924. This suited Hitler very well. He
had given instructions to Alfred
Rosenberg, who had succeeded Eckart
as editor of the *Völkischer Beobachter*
in the summer of 1923, to hold the
Party together during its official
dissolution. It was a shrewd move.

Rosenberg was a dull but quarrelsome
man and a wholly inadequate leader.
Hitler had nothing to fear from him as
a usurper of power; but he could be
relied upon to cause enough dissension
among such leading Nazis as Röhm,
Ludendorff and Streicher to keep the
Party alive with petty jealousies and
puny struggles for influence.

At a political level the forbidden
Party was kept afloat by the simple
means of fastening to it the name of
another ship – the National Socialist
German Freedom Movement, which
towed it through the national elections of April and May 1924 and indeed
won some two million votes and
thirty-two seats in the Reichstag (two
of them went to Röhm and Ludendorff).
Hitler was far from pleased by that
and was careful to aggravate the
quarrels among Party members so
that when more elections were held in
December dissension among the Nazis
had become so marked that they lost
half their votes and eighteen of their

Reichstag seats. This naturally comforted the government, which had been thinking seriously of having Hitler deported back to Austria. In exchange for Hitler's official resignation as leader of a movement that no longer officially existed he was released from Landsberg and allowed once more to practice politics. 'We no longer have anything to fear from a party in which so few have any confidence,' said the Minister of Justice.

The resuscitated *Völkischer Beobachter* appeared on 26th February 1925. A fortnight earlier Ludendorff had resigned from the Party. Eckart had died while Hitler was in prison; Göring was skulking in Sweden; Rosenberg was sulking; Röhm was being argumentative about leadership of the Storm Troopers (the argument was to lead to his forced resignation in April). And Hitler said unequivocally in his editorial that he intended to re-found the Party only on condition that he had undisputed leadership. (Nobody had in fact disputed his leadership, but his cunning in fostering Party quarrels had given the impression that he had many jealous rivals.)

Two days after the editorial he turned himself into a public figure again by convening a meeting of his supporters at the scene of his Pyrrhic victory the previous year – the Bürgerbräu Keller. The *Beobachter* reported that there were four thousand people present and that they rose to cheer Hitler 'as one man'.

Hitler's only noteworthy supporters on the platform were his publisher, Max Amann, and the faithful thug Julius Streicher, who said with remarkable ineptitude that the Führer's release was 'a gift from God'.

The Führer's speech lasted for two hours, which mercifully precludes its reproduction here except for a single brief extract:

'I alone lead the movement, and no one can impose conditions on me so long as I personally bear the responsibility. And I once more bear the whole responsibility for everything that occurs in the movement . . . To this struggle of ours there are only two possible issues: either the enemy pass over our bodies or we pass over theirs, and it is my desire that, if in the struggle I shall fall, the swastika banner shall be my winding sheet.'

That was a perfect cue for the dramatic flourishing of the Nazi banner that had been carried by Scheubner-Richter when he was shot outside the War Ministry on 9th November. The martyrdom myth had begun.

Not only the martyrdom but also, now, the *quasi* religious significance of the bullet-torn and bloodstained flag. 'This banner,' said Hitler, 'has now achieved the holiness of the Holy Grail. I shall personally see to it that it is used for the holiest of purposes – the consecration of those who link their fortunes, good or ill, with the struggles of the Fatherland.'

The speech, with its usual targets of

73

Jewish domination, the Marxist threat, and the Weimar republic, but with the earnest assurance that those forces would now be defeated by legal means rather than by the revolutionary *coup*, was a tremendous success. It was clear that he had lost none of his power to mesmerize an audience. But that same power had the effect of frightening the government, which quickly had second thoughts about having nothing to fear from the rebirth of the Nazi party. They issued an immediately effective Order in Council which, cleverly, did not subdue Party activities but forbade Hitler to address public meetings in most German states. (Ironically, one of the exceptions was Thuringia, the capital of which is Weimar.) Since Hitler was still on parole and had to consider the threat of deportation, the prohibition was not one he could ignore. It was to last until 1927. However, it was not likely that he would remain silent that long. Nor did he.

The country as a whole was edging toward industrial peace and political as well as financial stability. Field-Marshal von Hindenburg was elected to the Presidency in April 1925, and his democratic control ensured that disunity in the Reichstag was subdued almost to non-existence. There was, though, plenty among the Nazis. A splinter group had formed in north Germany and had been developed successfully by the brothers Otto and Gregor Strasser and a young man whose name was to become rather well known: Josef Göbbels. Gregor Strasser, unlike Hitler, was allowed to speak in public when and where he liked, and speak he did, often and effectively. But his message was far from being the one Hitler wanted to put across as Nazi doctrine. It was a message urging the acquisition of industry and property by the state, and it had too much Marxist tinge to

A young man whose name was to become well known: Josef Göbbels

please Hitler the demagogue, who relentlessly followed the path to personal power. But he was skilful enough in his machinations to avoid showing his hand too soon. When it suited him he was as good at coaxing as he was at browbeating; and he took his time and moved warily. It says much for his subtlety and patience that by the middle of 1926 he had effectively bridged the rift in the Party and won to his side the Strassers' firmest supporter, Göbbels.

'Dear and revered Adolf Hitler!' Göbbels wrote, in a letter of birthday greetings, 'I have learned so much from you! In your comradely fashion you have shown me fundamentally new ways which have finally made me see the light. The day may come when everything will go to pieces, when the mob around you will foam and grumble and roar, "Crucify him!". Then we shall stand firmly and unshakably and we will shout and sing, "Hosanna!".'

Not surprisingly, the lickspittle who could commit such nauseating twaddle to a letter could also confide to his diary:

'Adolf Hitler, I love you because you are both great and simple. These are the characteristics of genius. You have discovered the final form of German socialism. You will be able to turn the world upside down. Up in the sky a cloud takes the shape of a swastika. A flickering light shines in the heavens. It cannot be a star. Perhaps a signal of fate? These days have shown me the way and the direction. I feel at peace with myself. Now my last doubts have vanished. Germany shall live! Heil Hitler!'

With the Strassers' rivalry diminished the time had come for the breaking of silence, for an examination of the possibilities of another demonstration of the pageantry of power. Nearly three years had passed since the first Nuremberg rally; and now Nuremberg was out of bounds to Hitler as a public speaker. But a rally was planned all the same. Not inappropriately, at Weimar.

The rally of ideas

Apart from the fact that Hitler was permitted to speak there, Weimar had few of the attractions of Nuremberg as a rally centre. There were no conveniently placed big open spaces except the Marktplatz, which was not really big enough to manoeuvre huge forces in properly. Most of the assemblies would have to be held in restaurants and the German National Theatre, where the opportunities for pageantry were limited. However, since the rally was held mainly to

re-state the aims of the revived Party and to work out practical details of policy, the propaganda value of pageantry could to some extent be sacrificed.

This time the rally was called a Party Day. It began at four o'clock on the afternoon of Saturday 3rd July with a two-hour meeting of a Special Committee (the indefinite article serves: there were nine committees specializing in subjects varying from women to finance), and ended at mid-night next day with 'social congress' in the public gardens. The social congress, form unspecified, was conducted in heavy rain but was reported to be 'gaily successful'. Between the first Special Committee and the rain-swept gala in the gardens there were welcoming ceremonies in three different restaurants, the spectacular arrival of beflagged special trains from Sachsen and Munich, parades

Hitler's women and children

headed by those peculiarly German bands that specialize in brassy oom-pom-pom music, the ceremony of the Consecration of the Flags, mass demonstrations of Party Unity, a somewhat surprisingly entitled lecture on 'The Christian Moral Foundations of National Socialism', display marching by the Storm Troopers and *Stoss Truppe Hitler* (Hitler's personal bodyguard and shock troops), and of course the other eight Special Committees, at which policy decisions were wrought.

Streicher and Liebel were again in charge of the whole rally but this time they had assisting them a man called Viktor Lutz, a keen Storm Trooper who was to rise to the dizzy heights of Chief of Staff of that rabble-rousing organization. He was good looking in a playboy way, but harsh-voiced and unpopular except among his armbanded platoons of hoodlums, whom he drilled swaggeringly. Also on the Party Day organizing staff were Artur Dintner, *Gauleiter* of Thuringia, and his deputies Ernst Ziegler and Fritz Sauckel. Between them this sextet gained for the first rally of the reborn Party a great deal of attention. Much of it was antagonistic, but it was attention all the same.

Limited though the possibilities for pageantry were, much was done. The special trains draped with swastika banners had been musically welcomed at every station *en route* and pompous speeches were addressed to the passengers by civic officials standing on decorated podiums before the trains steamed out. All the Bavarian delegates and Party members – there were 2,000 of them – were dressed in leather shorts and embroidered braces and marched from the Weimar railway station with rhythmic knee-slapping gestures as if they were the chorus of 'White Horse Inn'. 'The sun glinting on their Party medals,' the *Beobachter* said, 'made a rich attestation to loyalty.' Well chosen words. The medals were an obligatory purchase, at fifty pfennigs each, by everyone attending, and the pfennigs of course went to subsidize the cost of the rally.

The Consecration of the Flags this year was, at Liebel's suggestion, given an air of secrecy. The ceremony was held in the German National Theatre at seven o'clock on Sunday morning, and only Storm Troopers and the tiny bodyguard of *Stoss Truppe* were allowed to attend. A great deal of descriptive information was allowed to leak out, however; and that was almost as successful at arousing passionate emotions among the non-participating public as their presence would have been. The solemnity of the occasion was given as the reason for permitting only the *corps d'élite* to take part. 'The Nazi banner carried by Doctor of Engineering Max Erwin von Scheubner-Richter in the *putsch* of 9th November 1923, ripped by the bullets of the opponents of the Party and hallowed by his blood as he fell in loyal faith in the resurrection of the German people, is henceforth to be called the Blood Banner of the Party, and its touch will make sacred the flag of every branch that springs from the flourishing tree of National Socialism.' So said the official programme.

The Storm Troopers were twice reviewed by Hitler. Uniformed now in belted breeches, brown shirts with swastika armbands, jackboots and visored soft caps, they paraded in companies for inspection by Hitler and later in the day marched past him as he stood in his open Mercedes wearing the shabby belted raincoat that had become his sartorial shibboleth. Both reviews were accompanied by band music, and the *Rienzi* overture was again played every time Hitler entered a hall.

So much for pageantry. But the proclamation convening the rally had plainly stated that 'Only mass demonstrations and a show of unity and strength are intended by the parades and ceremonies; the inner purpose of

'Only a show of unity and strength are intended by the parades'

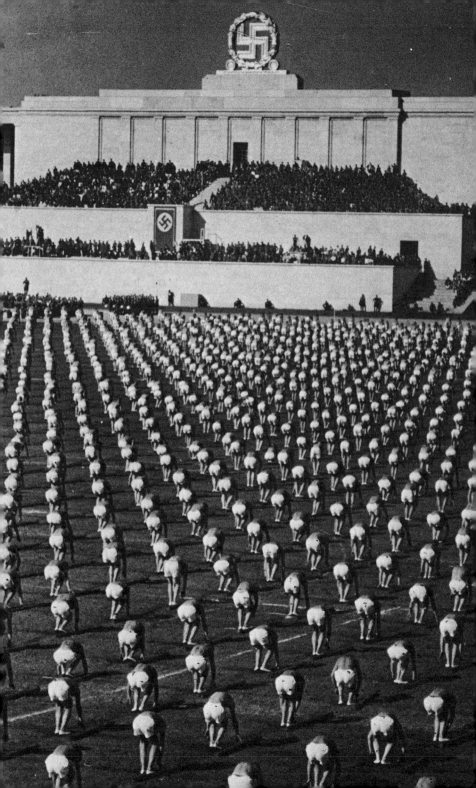

Above: **Propaganda speech**
Right: **Party meeting**

Party Day is as a congress of delegates meeting in Special Committees with the object of giving new incentive and direction to the movement'.

Leaving aside the Special Committees concerned with, for example, 'Problems Concerning Elections', 'Community Delegates', 'Civil Servants', 'Finance', and 'Labour unions', which were so to speak of mainly internal interest, there were others that did indeed give new incentive and direction to the Party. The most important and far reaching in their effects were those that formulated new plans for propaganda, youth, and women.

At the meeting concerned with propaganda, held in the Armbrust restaurant between seven and ten o'clock on the Saturday night, Dr Josef Göbbels began his approach to the road that led him to the Ministry

of that influential craft. It is an appropriate moment to give him and his methods a glance of consideration.

In 1926 he was twenty-nine years old, a Rhinelander, small in stature and with a faulty thigh bone that had been operated on for osteomyelitis when he was a child – an operation that had left him with one leg shorter than the other by four inches. He was sensitive to the point of mania about his physical deformity and concocted complex stories of war injuries to account for the crippled leg. (He had in fact volunteered for service in 1916 and understandably had been rejected as unfit.) He took a craftsman's pleasure in constructing such stories as if they belonged to the plot of a novel in which no weak spots must reveal themselves to eagle-eyed readers; and he was always adept at explaining away, with ever more complex lies, any discrepancies that might be detected. That ability was the heart of his talent as a propagandist.

Göbbels' education was reasonably good. He had attended a number of universities and earned his Doctorate with a thesis on – not inappropriately – Romantic Drama. He had worked as a secretary and publicist to the Strassers, and he recognized in Hitler a master propagandist. The chapter on the subject in the second volume of *Mein Kampf*, which Hitler had shown him in galley proof, was in Göbbels' opinion a brilliant analysis of the possibilities of 'a carefully built up erection of statements which, whether true or false, can be made to undermine quite rigidly held ideas and to construct new ones that will take their place. It would not be impossible to prove, with sufficient repetition and psychological understanding of the people concerned, that a square is in fact a circle. What, after all, are "square" and "circle"? They are mere words, and words can be moulded until they clothe ideas in disguise'.

As it happened, Hitler needed just such a clothier of ideas. Propaganda

was a full time job to which he could give only part of his time. He had therefore accepted Göbbels' smarmy compliments and fawning devotion and ordered him to speak on the subject at Weimar. Hitler himself took the chair and was immensely impressed by the smooth, musical voice of the little Rhinelander, and by his malicious wit and cynical intelligence. Göbbels was obviously having a similar effect on the audience. He saved for the climax of his address, in which he analyzed the relative effectiveness of press, poster, and speech, his conviction that the new medium, radio, was most important. 'In that medium,' he concluded, 'we have a great potential for influencing public opinion. I prophesy the day when every factory, every cinema and theatre and restaurant, every market place and store, every railway station, and every home will be within range of the Führer's voice.'

Nothing could have pleased Hitler more than the thought of a whole nation – perhaps even the world – listening to him. He closed the meeting with a eulogy on Göbbels' talents such as he seldom gave to anybody in public.

Several of the less enthusiastic Weimar newspapers detected a glint of danger in the prophecy of mass hypnotism by radio. The words *hinterlistig* and *heimtuckisch* (crafty, mischievous, insidious) were much used – rather as, in the 1950s, 'subliminal' advertising was opposed. It was exactly the reaction Hitler wanted. The opposition were revealing fear – a weakness that was always worth capitalizing. 'The Führer told me of of his approval of my plans to use the increasingly popular radio method of communication,' Göbbels wrote in his diary, 'and I am half crazy with pride that such a genius should see eye to eye with me into the future.'

The future was also the mainspring of the meeting concerning itself with youth. It was conducted by Streicher, who was still a schoolmaster – and by

all accounts a successful one if success is to be measured by popularity. He was aged thirty in 1926 and encouraged bullying and persecution among the older boys in his flock – especially if with unerring instinct he detected homosexual tendencies in them. (He was not himself homosexual; sadism and pornography were his sexual corners.) The price of his silence, when he discovered them *flagrante delicto*, which he often did by way of information furnished by victims of his tutorial punishments who preferred spy work to beating, was the humiliation of the smaller and more tremulous schoolboys. Among these the Jews, or suspected Jews, of course suffered the most extreme humiliations – including the cleansing of true German anuses with the tongue and the licking up of ordure and urine in the latrines. The masterful tendencies latent in this fine strain of German youth were well served by such licence and Streicher became a gubernatorial

The Führer speaking in committee; behind him the blood banner

hero to many of his pupils. His hefty stature and sneering arrogance also were greatly admired and imitated as the personification of masculinity. Clearly he was just the man to lead the young manhood of Germany.

Which in effect he did. For he, like Göbbels, put forward, at the meeting on education and youth, an idea that was to develop into one of the firmest structures of Nazism: the Hitler Youth Organization.

In embryo the Hitler Youth was to be disguised much as the Storm Troopers had been – as sports and physical fitness clubs so that the still prevailing Versailles conditions limiting the size of Germany's army could be given a reverential nod. Nobody was much deceived by that phoney obsequiousness, of which the *Morning Post* in due course remarked bluntly that 'the so-called Hitler Youth Organization is simply a breeding ground for the kind of thugs so beloved of Herr Göring and Herr

Himmler'. (Streicher eluded their condemnation for some reason or other.) But very many people were taken in by the notion of German Youth being drafted into compulsory labour service – also an idea first mooted by Streicher, who perhaps saw himself in hallucination as a colossus bestriding the slaves of a galley and whipping them into blood-stained action.

'The initiation of a young labour corps,' Streicher said, 'would have far-reaching economic benefits. The young people of today's Germany would learn devotion to German ideals and would at the same time be able to undertake great works of reconstruction, repair, irrigation and the like at small cost to the country because they would not need paying. Their reward would be the health of community life and the betterment of the Father-

land. My experience as an educationist is that there is great pressure from youth to serve the Fatherland.'

The idea was well received at the meeting by the small Special Committee empowered to scheme out the methods by which the country's manpower resources could be mustered and trained in a military sense; and when it developed during the next few years into the famous Labour Corps few among the Allies seem to have suspected a para-military organization lurking beneath the immensely successful engineering works – construction of autobahns, recovery of inundated land, bridge building and the like – that contributed so much to Germany's economic recovery. The *Morning Post*, commenting upon it, this time smiled with wiseacre approval and said it was 'a magnificent achievement untainted by the ulterior motives of Herr Hitler's military ambitions'. Herr Hitler's military ambitions were in fact well served by the martial training received at regular weekend camps which the Labour Corps were compelled to attend. Their reward, at later rallies, was for them to appear in their massed formations with their 40,000 spades glinting like rifles and receive the accolade of the Führer in one of his many long speeches devoted to the marvels of the German economy.

All that was of course some years ahead. For the time being the Labour Corps was no more than an idea with possibilities earnestly seized upon by the Special Committee for Education and Youth. In that it was like Göbbels' broadcasting prophecy: somewhat in advance of its time – radio still being in 1926 largely an affair of clumsy accumulators, complex tuning systems, tinny loudspeakers, headphones, crystal rectifiers, and short receiving ranges. But both notions were given their birth at the Weimar rally.

As also was the idea that German womanhood had a very special part to play in the structure of Nazism. The Order of German Women was given its start in the Ladies' Hall of the Armbrust restaurant at the same time (between 7.30 and 10am on Sunday 4th July) that Streicher was beating out the paths of the Hitler Youth and the Labour Corps in the adjoining Stage Room. Like all Nazi concepts it was clouded with the spurious idealism of a master race. But its practical aims were, first, to inculcate into the women of Germany a belief in the importance of pure Aryan blood, and secondly to encourage in their offspring by precept and example undeviating dedication to the Nazi cause.

At that rallying of the nation's women to the service of the Adolf Hitler stud farm some phrases of quite remarkable obviousness were used and later publicized by Göbbels as if they were newly turned out at the propaganda mint. Perhaps he convinced himself that they were; publicists need to believe in the product they are selling. The gems of the collection were: 'Women are the eternal mothers of the nation'; 'Women are the eternal companions of men in work and battle'; 'The triumphant task of women is to bear and tend babies'; and 'Men are willing to fight, but when they are wounded women must be there to nurse them'. All Germany was to become familiar with those slogans; and to take them seriously too. At the most perilous time of the war, in Hamburg during the British bombing, the ace reporter Chester Wilmot overheard two German women meeting, greeting, commiserating with each other, and parting with the salutation 'Well, our Führer says we are the eternal mothers of the nation and we must be proud that he had made us so'. And that without a trace of irony.

The Weimar rally, then, was a spawning ground for some of the ideas that from 1927 on were to become decorated with the full pageantry of power.

Recruits

The city waits

Nuremberg's medieval architecture, like the poetry of Mrs E W Wilcox, is a matter of taste. 'Those who like this sort of thing will find this the sort of thing they like,' as Max Beerbohm said in another connection. The young English tourist already quoted who arrived and departed on the eve of the 1923 rally and found 'much inspiration for the imagination' among the elaborately decorated gables and pinnacles was by no means the first to do so. But his enthusiasm was restrained compared with that of two jolly German wanderers, Ludwig Tieck and Heinrich Wackenroder, who

clearly were literary ancestors of Dr Göbbels' lyrical syrup, and who wrote an account of their discovery of the town in 1797. A small dose of it goes a long way:

'O Nuremberg, thou once world famous city! With what child-like eyes did I revel at thy quaint houses and churches which bear the visible imprint of our old patriotic art! How dearly do I love the creations of that time which speak such an outright powerful and true language. How do they lure me back into that great century, when thou, Nuremberg, were the lively throbbing school of our national art and a fertile overflowing spirit lived and worked within thy walls.'

The book was called *Die Herzensergiessungen eines Kunst-liebenden Klosterbruders*, which will surprise no one, and it acted on the early 19th-century German public like a high-pressure sales campaign. Nuremberg was rediscovered. Epics and myths of history were decorated with as many curlicues as the tall gables of the

The burning of books was part of the fanatical Nazi suppression of 'unwelcome' propaganda

buildings and re-presented. All the famous sons of the town had their reputations burnished. The songs and poems of the 12th-century Minnesingers – troubadours who were based at the Nuremberg court of Frederick II – were counted as the nucleus of Franconian culture. Such names as Tannhaüser, Wolfram, Vogelweide, emerged from the dust of legend; and to them were added the artisans Borkhardt and Gerler, who made organs and lutes. It was suddenly remembered that Albrecht Dürer had been born here and a great scurrying about to find some of his pictures went on; but to little avail. Most of them had been sold with mercenary glee by the town council into whose hands they fell after Dürer's death in 1528. Stricken conscience, however, had inspired the Nurembergers with a pious devotion to the preservation of his house near the Thiergärtnerthor, which throughout the 19th century was an object of tourists' reverence.

Hans Sachs also was rediscovered. Sachs was a cobbler turned literary man who became more famous in the part created for him by Wagner in *Die Meistersinger* than he was in real life. But he had local fame while he lived, which was long enough (1494-1576) to enable him to produce more than six thousand plays, songs, poems, essays and fables. The Mastersingers of Sachs' day were a guild of songsters who based their activities on the Minnesingers' but gradually channelled their song contests into a maze of increasingly pedantic rules that reached the stage in 1646, of a volume entitled *The Nuremberg Funnel for Pouring in all the Essence of the Art of German Poetry and Rhyme in Six Lessons*. It was this pedantry that Wagner mocked in *Die Meistersinger* by making Sachs recognize the poetic worth of Walter's prize song even though it does not conform to the rule of the contest.

'The Mastersingers of Nuremberg' was first performed in 1876 and its

Heinrich Himmler in melodramatic posture

instant popularity set a crown of fame upon the historical and artistic trappings of the town over which the beaming hikers Tieck and Wackenroder had burbled lyrically eight years earlier. The denigratory term 'culture vulture' had not been coined in 1876, but no matter; historians phoney and otherwise flocked upon the place. It was fitted out with marvels of Germanic accoutrements that fell with the crash of heavily dropped names. It was not enough that Attila and Barbarossa and Charlemagne had fought in the place. Evidence had to be discovered or planted to prove that the castle had once been a temple of Diana, that there was another ancient god, Nuoro, who gave his name to the rituals performed there and subsequently by extension to the town, and that Tiberius Claudius established a Roman colony within the fortress walls. Blinded as it was by such philological and historical dazzle, the nation made of Nuremberg a place of virtually holy pilgrimage.

But whimsy too was plastered thickly on. Toymaking, since medieval times one of Nuremberg's flourishing industries, was particularly adaptable in that direction. And whimsy like culture can form part of a sinister deception, as if one were to peer behind the façade of Mrs Wilcox's innocent platitudes and discover there the draft of a fully fledged plan for the extermination of a nation.

Which is indeed not so far from the truth. For by 1927, when the next Nazi rally was held in Nuremberg, there was already sequestered behind the elaborate mystique of legend and whimsy, along the cobbled lanes, beneath the overhanging gables, the brooding threat of genocide. Julius Streicher and Dr Artur Dintner, Gaulieter of Thuringia, were between them concocting the practical details of the anti-Semitic doctrine that was soon to be officially adopted.

Day of awakening

er
indenburg wählt
ilft den Nazis!

Am 3. Dezember 1931 schrieb der „Vorwärts":
„Wenn die Nationalsozialisten die Spielregeln der Demokratie beachten, sind wir alle bereit, sie lieber heute wie morgen an die Regierung heranzulassen"

roener handelt also ganz
Sinne der SPD., wenn er
tzt Hitlers SA. in die Reichs-
ehr einmarschieren läßt!

SPD.-Arbeiter! Wie hieß es 1925?
„Der Kandidat der Reaktion heißt Hindenburg" „Vorwärts", 14. April 1925

2 MILLIARDEN JÄHRLICHE TRIBUTLAS

Also present in Nuremberg in 1927 was a Nazi headed for high Party office, one who was to have more to do with the execution than the adoption of the anti-Semitic doctrine that Streicher and Dintner were so busily working out. Not that one would have known at the time that so horribly distinguished a career lay ahead of him. In fact one really hardly noticed him at any time. Heinrich Himmler was a man whom it pleased to remain unnoticed. He was a man who listened, watched, lurked invisibly, compiled dossiers of information. No one could have been better cut out to be a secret policeman. The Gestapo had not yet been formed, but here without doubt was its promising executive.

He was at that time twenty-seven years old, modest in manner, small in stature, indefinite in feature, mild in expression, a most unmemorable man. He had studied agriculture in Munich, failed to get his degree, and was now working as a laboratory assistant in a Munich chemical plant that manufactured fertilizers. His greatest talent, which he had so far had little

Nazi election posters

opportunity of demonstrating, was for organization.

The enormity of Himmler's crimes as a genocidal maniac was to become hideously evident in the concentration camps of Buchenwald and Belsen. But his instinct was always toward concealment. He was a man of the shadows. It is therefore difficult to report with any accuracy on his furtive activities in Nuremberg in 1927. However, it is established that on 24th February he arrived at an unpretentious guest-house in Egideienplatz and remained there for six days 'going daily to Mass in St. Egidius' church.' The proprietors of the guest-house were Andreas Kulmbach and his wife, and it was they who noted his regular church attendance. Kulmbach was a toymaker specializing in hand carved puppets and the window on to the *platz* was filled with the brightly coloured wooden dolls. It is perhaps not without ironic significance that

the man who, after the attempted assassination of Hitler in 1944, became the acknowledged master of Germany, once hid behind the façade of a puppet shop.

It is also established that during his week in Nuremberg he conferred several times with Streicher and Eintner, though it is by no means certain who sent for him or why. He was an insignificant member of the Party who had served in the infantry from 1917 to 1919 and had taken part in the Munich *putsch*. He was a protégé of Gregor Strasser rather than of Hitler, and perhaps for that reason is not mentioned in *Mein Kampf*.

However he came to be there, he proved to be of great value to Streicher, 'a man in whose knowledge there are gaps as wide as the Zeppelin-wiese' he noted in the dossier he was already compiling on *Gauleiter* Streicher. His magpie instinct for the

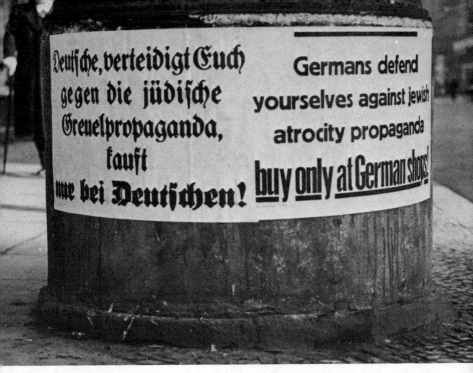

Anti-Jewish propaganda

collection and collation of information was put to practical use during the week by bridging some of the gaps in the *Gauleiter's* knowledge of the history of the Jews in Nuremberg. He was able to provide a most satisfying précis of that history – a précis that had sinister effects on the draft of the doctrinal muniment Streicher was preparing.

'A remarkably thorough man,' Dintner recorded. 'He had with him sheaves of neatly ordered papers from which he could quote unfailingly chapter and verse for all his references. Rindfleisch's massacre of Nuremberg's Jews in 1298 for the desecration of the Host we all knew about. But he went to book after book and opened our eyes to many other possibilities.'

There were indeed considerable possibilities to be exploited. In Nuremberg's history Jews had been sold as slaves, taken in pawn, presented as gifts from bishop to emperor. They had been kidnapped and ransomed for fortunes, banished outside the city walls, forbidden to conduct business, led round the town on ropes by leprous beggars, forced into brothels, taxed, maimed, flung to the moat from the castle ramparts. Their synagogues had many times been burnt to the ground, their fortunes confiscated. The merchant guilds, however, found that too few Jews meant poverty in the town, since there was no one else to extort taxes from, and they were encouraged back again – but only as merchants, not as residents.

That was in the 16th century. Every Jew had to present himself at the gates of the city and buy a yellow Star of David, which was his passport for the day. Another tax was payable at the customs house for a disease-ridden hag past her time in the brothels, who would fling a halter round his neck and lead him to the place where business was to be done. Further taxes were payable when he left the city gates, and if his business overran its time so that he passed the curfew hour and was forced to stay

Left: Jewish quarter, 1933. *Above:* The consecration with the Blood Banner

overnight, a very substantial sum had to be paid in addition for a special permit.

Three hundred years passed before, in 1839, a single Jew, Joseph Wassermann, was given permission to live in the town. From then on their rights were grudgingly extended until they were on more or less equal footing with non-Jewish Nurembergers.

The more successful of these newly established Jewish residents were surprisingly generous considering they had so much of an ungenerous nature to remember, and devoted much of their time and money to art, medicine, and social services. Dr Alec Frankenburger spent his life and most of his money working out schemes for the aid of tuberculous children; Eugen Herz established a society for feeding and sheltering the destitute; Wilhelm von Gerngros, Sigmund Pickert, Heinrich Berolzheimer, Siegfried Bach, and Michel Kahn were all patrons of the arts.

All this and much more Himmler gave in copious detail to Streicher and Dintner. A great deal of it was inspiring. Why should not history repeat itself? It should not be impossible once more to persecute Jews beyond the limit of tolerance, and at the same time to fatten Nuremberg's treasury with taxes and levies. Even more satisfactory, it might not even be beyond achievement to exterminate the Jewish race altogether.

Since no record other than Dintner's observation of Himmler's thoroughness exists, it is impossible to state how or by whom the proposed solution to 'the Jewish problem' was worked out. But incontrovertibly there appeared in the *Völkischer Beobachter* the following week a 'Five-point plan to diminish the influence of Judaism'. The five points were briefly and lucidly made:

'The citizenship of every Jew in

Above right: The secret policeman: Himmler. *Right:* Nuremberg 1928: the march past

Germany to be revoked so that no voting or other rights remain to them; no Jew to be permitted to teach, administer the law, or work in government posts; no marriage between Jews and Aryans to be permitted and non-marital sexual intercourse to be punished with death for the Jew concerned; the purchase of any German land or building to be forbidden to Jews; all Jews immigrant to Germany after 1914 to be expelled and their property confiscated.'

Having contributed to the working out of this uncharitable proposal, Himmler disappeared from the Nuremberg scene for some time. The evidence of his work, however, manifested itself not only in the publication of the 'Five-point plan', but also in other ways. Several Jews were imprisoned on trumped-up charges. Buildings and statues that had been given to the town by Herz, Gerngros, Pickert, Berolzheimer, Kahn and other Jews were tarred and feathered, scrawled over with the huge word *Jüde*, or crudely decorated with yellow Stars of David. There were of course many protests in newspapers and at public meetings. In 1927 it was still possible to protest. The Grand Hotel even went to the length of refusing to accommodate any declared Nazi. But Streicher and his like knew only too well that they would not have to wait very long. History was repeating itself. The pogrom had begun.

So far as dramatic spectacle was concerned the three-day rally held in August was ineffective. There was no flood-lighting of the castle, very little decoration of the town, no evident enthusiasm following the swastika. The increasing economic stability of the country had raised the popularity of the Weimar government and extremists were out of favour. All the same, the number of Party members had more than doubled since the Weimar rally. There were now 50,000 of them. Followers of the Party as distinct from actual members probably totalled another 100,000. The Nazi

Beobachter claimed 160,000 arriving to attend the rally from all over Germany in forty-seven trains; the opposition said the demonstration was small-scale and that 'only a few thousand followers of Hitler, wearing uniforms and medals, attended the rally'. The truth probably lay between the two.

The spectacular side of the pro-

gramme was limited to a torchlight parade through the Nuremberg streets, the 'Blood Banner' ceremony (held in the open air this time) and several brass band concerts. For the rest, as at the Weimar rally, there was a great deal of tub thumping by Göbbels, Streicher, and of course Hitler – who had had the ban on his public speaking lifted and put forward not only the 'Five-point plan' (and thereby established official Nazi doctrine) but also voiced his opinions on the need for increased population of a 'pure' strain and for more room to put these pure

Göbbels, Göring and Hitler watch the approach of another rally contingent

new people in. It was not the last time the word *lebensraum* was used.

The scene of the larger assemblies was either the Zeppelinwiese or the Luitpoldhain. Both these big open spaces had been used largely as dumping grounds and they had to be cleared of heaps of old scrap iron before anything could happen in them. Streicher and Liebel organized the clearance very efficiently. All Jews who had been convicted of civil offences – and the number increased surprisingly between February and August – worked out their sentences in a forced labour corps that was engaged twenty-four hours a day in clearance. At night batteries of Kleig lights illuminated the scene with its sweating prisoners, overseers with truncheons drawn, and endless lines of wagons taking the scrap away. 'From this scene,' Streicher reported to Hitler, 'I decided on similar illuminations for our rallies of the future.'

Considering that on the face of things the Party was at a low ebb in its popularity in 1927, the rally was truthfully recorded as being 'highly successful. There is a strong heart beating in the National Socialist party. We have reached a day of awakening'. So wrote Dr Göbbels.

There was one more Nazi rally in the Twenties, in 1929. The previous year was a disastrous one for the Party in the Reichstag: they held only twelve of the 491 seats, having polled fewer than a million votes in the 1928 elections. But the Party membership rose steadily to 60,000 by the end of the year and there was much strengthening of its new offshoots the *Schülerbund* or School Children's League, the Students' League, the Order of German Women, and the Unions of Nazi Lawyers and Physicians. These branches put down roots that ran unhindered below the surface and were of immense value to both Dr Göbbels

Above right: Contingent of storm troopers from Berlin. *Right:* Young Nazis, 1925

and Herr Himmler when in due course they crept upon the upper crust scene again.

Göbbels had been disappointed of the job of propaganda chief, which he had been reasonably led to expect Hitler had given it to Gregor Strasser, his erstwhile opponent for leadership of the Party, instead. That was in October 1926, soon after the Weimar rally at which Göbbels made his striking début. The reason for Hitler's choice mystified as well as angered Göbbels. He had not yet learned to understand the cunning with which Hitler played his executives off against each other so that their personal jealousies should deflect them from challenging his leadership. All the same, Hitler could not afford to have embittered men in the higher echelons of the Party – particularly if they were men with unquestionable talents. On 26th October Göbbels was appointed *Gauleiter* of Berlin.

Leadership of the Party in the capital city was a very important post and Göbbels made the most of it. He excised the corrupt streak in the organization by expelling 400 members, got himself involved in libel suits that could never be made to stick but were excellent Nazi propaganda, started a newspaper called *Der Angriff*, initiated effective smear campaigns against the Deputy Chief of Police, who was Jewish, and gained from the Berlin electorate one of the twelve Nazi seats in the Reichstag. (The others included those held by Gregor Strasser and Hermann Göring, who had recently returned from his hideout in Sweden.) Hitler had every reason to be pleased, and was.

On 9th January 1929 there was a reshuffling of the Nazi 'cabinet'. Strasser was made Chief of Organization and Deputy Führer, and Göbbels slipped at last into his predestined niche: Reich Chief of Propaganda. His first act was to set in motion the plans for the spectacular 1929 rally.

The first Nazi soap opera

Max Reinhardt, the producer of spectacular theatrical epics, would have been ideal as the guiding genius behind the Nuremberg rallies. There is a crude newspaper strip cartoon of the time showing Göbbels approaching him wearing the grin of a Cheshire cat and clutching bags of money. He discovers in the second frame that Reinhardt is Jewish, his real name Goldmann, and the cat grin is transformed in the last frame into the hideous beak of a vulture. But Jew though Reinhardt was and therefore contemptible to the Nazis, his ideas were there for the plucking, and it was with his kind of

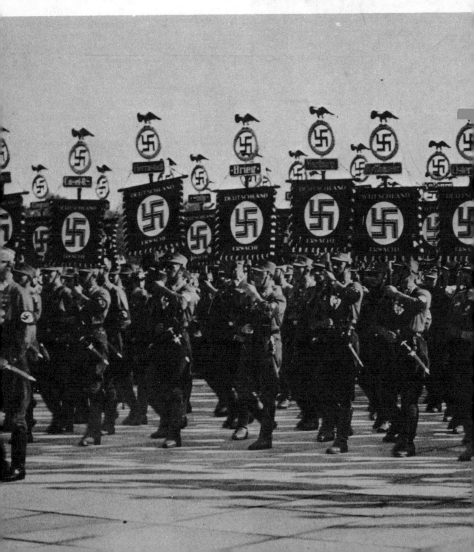

prodigal hand that the 1929 rally was organized. Here were to be seen for the first time the adaptation of opera, drama and cinema techniques that were to prove so successful.

Somewhat surprisingly in view of the emphasis on dramatic spectacle, the theme of the rally was 'Composure'. Whether the composure referred to was the smug indifference with which the Nazis viewed their seemingly weakening hold on the electorate it is impossible to say. There was in any case little evidence of anything but stridency, action, music.

At eleven o'clock on the morning of 2nd August a blaring fanfare of trumpets marked the beginning of the rally. The trumpeters stood in two ranks outside the Kulturvereinshaus, gonfalons embroidered with swastikas fastened to their silvered trumpets. They were answered by echoing fanfares in the reclaimed arenas of the Zeppelinwiese and Luitpoldhain. One of the Zeppelin Company's freight airships passed over the Zeppelinwiese – so-called because of its earlier use as a landing ground by the in-

Advance of the regimental contingents across the Luitpoldhain arena, 1934

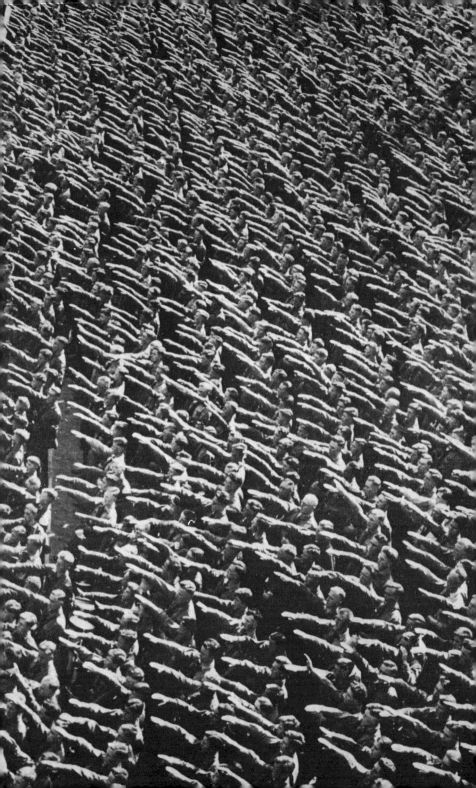

Left: Hitler youth, Nuremberg 1934. *Above:* Honour to the Munich martyrs

defatigable aircraft constructor – and showered down upon it basket after basket of rose petals. His arrival perfectly timed, Hitler's open tourer drew up before the Kulturvereinshaus as the fanfares ended. This time he had discarded the grubby trench coat and wore the Party uniform of brown shirt, breeches and jackboots. By 1929 public address equipment was well developed, and as Hitler entered the hall a recorded version of the inevitable *Rienzi* overture played by Furtwängler and the Berlin Philharmonic brought the 2,000 delegates to their feet. Mounting the dais, the Führer was ushered into the seat on the right of the Chairman, Gregor Strasser, while his bodyguard of *Stoss Truppe* lined up at the rear of the dais and immediately in front of it – 'their helmeted heads silhouetted like footlights against the brilliantly lighted stage with its drapings of black, red and white silk and the floodlit swastika surmounted by a huge symbolic eagle.'

This impressive bit of hocus-pocus was followed by Streicher's official speech of welcome and Hitler's proxy, Adolf Wagner, who read the Führer's opening speech for him, thus saving the precious voice for later and more worthy occasions. Streicher, in an army uniform he was not entitled to wear, flourished his whip and Wagner turned the leaves of his script as if they were the leaves of holy writ. The speeches that filled the rest of the session went on for hours. Dr Göbbels on 'Propaganda as the Key to Political Power' in eighty brisk minutes was the briefest of the speakers.

Once or twice ugly incidents threatened when ex-service men (*Reichsbannermen*) heckled and the line of *Stoss Truppe* in front of the stage moved silently forward, and silently delivered rabbit punches to the hecklers, and frog-marched the inert bodies through the exits. The speakers never faltered in their delivery. The rest of the *Reichsbannermen* remained speechless; but there were some mysterious deaths of Storm Troopers who were knifed while solitarily threading their way through the darker back streets that night. Those deaths were not reported in the *Völkischer Beobachter*.

Next day, as dusk gathered over the vast Zeppelinwiese, the first of the great lamp-lit dramas began. A crowd of 150,000 had made their way on foot and by public transport to the arena. Shuttle services of trains and coaches had been running all day, perfectly on time and with 'crowd monitors' shepherding the people aboard as if they were components being eased down a conveyor belt toward an assembly point. Flags fell, turnstiles clicked, people were chopped off in fifties and fed into the arena. Precisely at eight o'clock the distant sound of *Deutschland uber Alles* could be heard. As the band approached the stadium two athletes carrying burning torches ran through the gates. They took up positions in the corners farthest from the entrance. They were followed by others, dozens of them, who lined up round the edges of the field. By the time the band arrived and marched in the arena was ablaze with the smoking torches. The band played on, a jigsaw of dramatic phrases from Beethoven, Wagner, Brahms, cunningly arranged to conclude with the final pages of the *Tannhäuser* overture. As the music blared to its end the torches were simultaneously extinguished on a cue from the bandmaster and the floodlights were switched on. The bandsmen stood alone in the centre of the arena and all the torchbearers now moved with absolute precision to surround them and form a solid phalanx.

No one could have called it ineffective. The crowd roared its approval. The torchbearers, clad in white (for Youth of course) went through more complex drill movements and ended up by forming a human swastika with the bandsmen at the centre.

Serried ranks of SS in the Luitpoldhain 1935

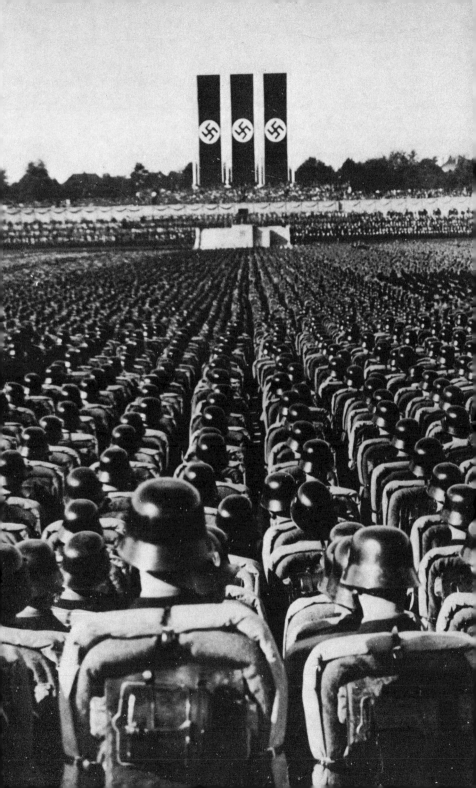

Ohne Brechung der W

Streicher making a bitter anti-Jewish speech in the arena, Nuremberg

Parade through Nuremberg, 1934

rrschaft der Juden, kein We

Above: Saluting base, Nuremberg 1935. *Below:* March of the political leaders, Nuremberg 1935. *Right:* SS guards beneath the Nazi eagle that typified the Nuremberg decorative symbols

Left: Overture to the soap opera
Above: Hess speaks, Hitler listens,
Luitpoldhalle, Munich

Göbbels then introduced Hitler, who seemingly no longer felt called upon to save his voice and spoke for nearly two hours on – what else? – the evils of Versailles, the Weimar republic, and the existing order of Jewish-controlled finance that was slowly blistering Germany into economic ruin. In demolishing the system that was in fact steadying the country's economy he was well aided by Göbbels, who had been particularly successful in providing the 'facts' that proved black to be white, a square a circle. 'Mere words,' one recalls him saying '[which] can be moulded until they clothe ideas in disguise.'

The disguised ideas were remorselessly hammered into the crowd's vulnerable eight o'clock wits until 9.50 when Hitler finally ceased his prating. As always, he had hypnotized them into acceptance by his personality while the hammer of his speech thudded on. And now, emotionally responding in turn to indignation, revenge, determination and triumph, they were regaled with the final spectacle of the evening.

The lights dimmed and huge frames of light wood were wheeled into place. Upon them were arranged pyrotechnical set pieces, and for an hour and a half now a dazzling display of land and naval battles was fought out in fireworks while star shells burst above the arena and rockets whizzed to their zenith over Nuremberg. The air was heavy with the acrid smell of gunpowder – 'the sharp smell of corruption', Alfred Nobel called it – and finally there bloomed high above the

arena an immense wreath of green bay leaves encircling a white plaque on which a fiery swastika glowed.

It was a great triumph – for Göbbels and Dr Ley who had schemed out the whole of the evening's presentation, and Sauer the pyrotechnist whose fireworks had concluded it so effectively. Göbbels slid again into the nauseating lyricism of a fawning cur when recording the event in his diary:

'Hitler, loved and gentle shepherd of the flock! Your praise for my pageant at Nuremberg was like honey in the draught of life! I grovel before thy mighty generosity, thy gift of thanks O Führer!'

One must of course pause to consider whether such sickening abasement in the private pages of a diary was intended only cynically. And indeed Göbbels in his public pronouncements often revealed a talent for cynical wit. But had irony been intended by thus privately apostrophizing a kind of Saint Hitler, its true significance could only have meant a secret enmity. In fact Göbbels' subsequent career proves that his devotion to Hitler never wavered, nor did his activities as the high priest of the cult of Nazism deviate by a millimetre from their course.

Whatever the impulse behind his private grovelling, Göbbels deserved thanks. The evening was climactic in its effect in spite of its occurring in the middle of the three-day rally instead of at the end. The remaining spectacular events were conventional in form: a ceremony at the new war memorial, the consecration of thirty-six new Party flags by the Blood Banner, parades by Storm Troopers and the Hitler Youth. The sound of marching feet echoed hour after hour through the streets, the massed crowds in the arenas could be heard for miles chanting rhythmically 'Germany, awaken'. But all that was by now hallowed custom. It was the new application of theatrical techniques

Homage to the dead, Luitpoldhain 1934

that made the rally memorable.

The memory had to last a long time. There were no more congresses at Nuremberg until 1933. That of course was the year of Hitler's attainment of complete power. The intervening time had too fully occupied the Nazis in their struggle for power for celebrations to be held. And the struggle had been an exhausting one in which the Party's fate had often been poised on a touch-and-go brink. Alan Bullock in his study of Hitler says that Nazi propaganda (meaning Dr Göbbels) 'Later built up a legend which represented Hitler's coming to power as the upsurge of a great national revival. The truth is more prosaic . . . Hitler did not seize power; he was jobbed into office by a backstairs intrigue.

'Far from being inevitable, Hitler's success owed much to luck and even more to the bad judgement of his political opponents and rivals. While the curve of Communist success at the elections continued to rise, the Nazis had suffered their sharpest set-back in November 1932, when they lost two million votes . . . .

'Before he came to power Hitler never succeeded in winning more than thirty-seven per cent of the votes in a free election. Had the remaining sixty-three per cent of the German people been united in their opposition he could never have hoped to become Chancellor by legal means; he would have been forced to choose between taking the risks of a seizure of power by force or the continued frustration of his ambitions. He was saved from this awkward dilemma by two factors: the divisions and ineffectiveness of those who opposed him, and the willingness of the German Right to accept him as a partner in governments.'

Professor Bullock says all that need be noted here of those intervening years. On 30th January 1933 Hitler became Chancellor of the German Reich. His power, as would soon be seen, was now absolute.

The formidable partnership

People who think of Horst Wessel – and there are probably remarkably few of them nowadays – usually think of a song; just as Struwwelpeter is thought of first as a caricature of a boy with unruly hair and long finger-nails. Horst Wessel was a man, of a sort; a considerably less endearing one than Struwwelpeter; and like Scheubner-Richter who carried the banner he entered the Nazi mythology by way of martyrdom. Göbbels made of him, first, an epitome of German youth and idealism, then, as events offered, a national hero.

Wessel joined the Party in 1926, aged nineteen. He was blond, physically magnificent, handsome, idle, brutal and amoral. He lived on the earnings of a whore called Erna Jaenicke,

Hitler and Rohm: memorial service

Left: Gauleiter Streicher honours the martyrs of Munich. *Above:* Hitler speaks in the Hofbräuhaus, Munich

having stolen her from her previous pimp, whose name was Ali Hoehler. Not unnaturally Hoehler was out for revenge; and a chance came when Erna's landlady, Frau Salm, resentful because Erna owed her rent, revealed to Hoehler where Erna and Wessel were to be found. He found them very quickly, shot Wessel through the mouth, seized Erna and escaped with her. That was on 14th January 1930. On 23rd February Wessel died, every lingering agony of his death having been reported by Göbbels in *Der Angriff*. 'Wherever there is a Germany, you will be, too, Horst Wessel!' he screamed in banner headlines after five weeks of wailing and gnashing his metaphorical teeth.

International Judaism was of course the murderer. 'Horst Wessel was murdered because he was a National Socialist,' Göbbels went on screaming.

There was no mention of Erna Jaenicke, Hoehler (who also in fact was a Nazi), or Frau Salm, which no doubt was very convenient for them. As things turned out, however, Hoehler was caught and his trial threatened the already burgeoning Horst Wessel legend. Fortunately the Storm Troopers under the direction of Himmler, who had by then been inducted into the Bavarian police, had no difficulty in finding Hoehler, Frau Salm and all the other witnesses and quietly murdering them. Thus the legend of the martyred hero was sustained undamaged.

He did a great deal more for the Nazi image as a dead pimp than he had ever done as a live Party member. He had written a short poem extolling the glories of National Socialism and it had been published in *Der Angriff* in September 1929. It fitted a traditional tune, and at Wessel's funeral Göbbels had the ingenious notion of having it sung as a threnody. Even more ingeniously, he established the tradi-

Left: Idealised sculpture of Horst Wessel. **Above:** Horst Wessel as a storm trooper: the propaganda picture

tion of a ghostly roll-call. 'Horst Wessel,' he called, and the assembled Storm Troopers replied *sotto voce*, 'Here'. No Nazi rally, and few smaller assemblies of Party members afterward took place without this ritual mumbo-jumbo; and the *Horst Wessel* song sank into the Nazi repertoire as deeply as 'Lili Marlene'.

In the ordering of such image-making Göbbels' talents were formidable. He could, and did, twist successful slogans out of anything. For example, the Dawes Plan, which was one of the chief boosters of Germany's economic recovery, was turned by Göbbels into a threatening evil by a slogan deriving from the letters of Dawes' name: *Deutchlands Armut Wird Ewig Sein* (Germany's poverty will last for ever). But slogans and the fabrication of martyrs were but the thin end of the wedge of his wizardry as a propagandist. He studied most carefully the techniques for the promotion

of film stars – then approaching their zenith in the heavens – and adapted them to the less glamorous pursuits of the Party leaders. Hitler himself was of course the star and he received what would nowadays be called 'the full treatment'. He travelled frequently by plane when air travel was a matter for publicity, had his photograph on every hoarding, appeared in films and magazines patting children's heads and caressing dogs, made gramophone records of election speeches, and displayed every agreeable facet of character from benevolence to invincible strength. Under Göbbels' internecine web of propaganda it gradually became impossible to move about, or even to stay at home, without being – to coin a verb – hitlered.

Thus by 1933 the entire nation had been hypnotized or bludgeoned into accepting Hitler and Nazism as the most powerful force in the country. Whether one agreed with the policy was of course a different matter. Support of the Party would take care of you one way, the Gestapo the other. Stephen Roberts in *The House that*

At the grave of Horst Wessel:
Above: 1935. *Right:* 1937

Hitler Built, published in 1937, says that the Gestapo:

'Watch every household in the land and pounce on opposition before it is organized, and unfortunately sometimes before it is even thought of. They override the law and punish as they think fit. In short, they are as untrammelled a race of young autocrats as the world has ever seen, and the very necessity for them, and the extraordinary range of their powers, throws much light on the real nature of Hitlerism.'

In 1933 the Gestapo, the State secret police, did not exist as such. What would become their job as thugs was still carried out by the Storm Troopers. But Himmler by now had under his control the black-shirted *Stoss Truppe*, which had been enlarged into a private police force, the *Shutz Staffeln* or SS. He was their Reichsführer as well as head of the Bavarian police, and was

busily compiling the dossiers on the leaders of the Storm Troopers and other political enemies who would later be liquidated by Hitler, having irritated him with their 'revolutionary' plans within the Party. The SS would supply the firing squads. Whether one calls them *Stoss Truppe*, *Schutz Staffeln*, SS or Gestapo, Himmler's black-shirted henchmen fulfilled the office of inquisitors. It was they who aroused households at midnight, departed with victims for 'interrogation', despatched the 'guilty' to Dachau, Belsen, Buchenwald. It was well to be on the side of the formidable partnership of the Party, to absorb Dr Göbbels' propaganda, to remember the authoritative presence of Reichsführer Himmler scanning through his rimless spectacles the accumulating 'evidence' against those who obstinately remained unconvinced of the probity of Nazi policy and the omnipotence of Hitler.

Microcosm of victory

The light shed for Mr Roberts on the real nature of Hitlerism by the Gestapo was shed in an actual luminary sense by the lights of Nuremberg in 1933. This was the Congress of Victory, a not altogether inappropriate theme-title considering the landslide triumph at the election and the achievement of the Chancellorship by Hitler. Rudolf Hess thought of the name – if it could be said to need any thinking of – and presented it with pathetic eagerness to Hitler. 'This, Führer, must be the greatest victory ever celebrated.'

It wasn't, but let that pass. What must not be allowed to pass is the observation that every known facet of Hitlerism was manifested at the Nuremberg rally of 1933 and at every one afterward. Even at the first truly spectacular rally in 1929 a certain

Massed salute to the banner

amount of restraint had been exercised. Those who, like the proprietors of the Grand Hotel, were on the wrong side of the Party line, were not physically assaulted unless it could be done without fear of police action (though no doubt many names were accumulated by the silently industrious Himmler for later use), and the persecution of Jews was kept mainly to cooked-up minor charges and petty humiliations like the labour gangs making ready the Zeppelinwiese and Luitpoldhain. But now, as one paper, *Der Montag*, put it 'A complete microcosm of the Reich was to be seen at Nuremberg during the days 31st August to 3rd September 1933.'

This time there was no restraint. 'The amount of intimidation in the city,' the *New York Times* man wrote, 'already great before the rally, is now enormously increased.' Jewish shops were forced to display the Star of David and Storm Troopers stood before them to prevent people entering. Sometimes they 'accidentally' poked

Above: The speaker. *Right:* The leader

their rifles through windows. 'The magic spell of the Master Race,' the *Völkischer Beobachter* said, using the grandiloquent title for what seems to be the first time, 'causes the inferiors to shudder and tremble and abase themselves before our Aryan superiority.' There was little magic about the jackbooted arrogance of Julius Streicher, who on his appointment as *Gauleiter* of Franconia had given up school-teaching and was now able to stride all day through Nuremberg and the other towns in his bailiwick, his whip at the ready. Nor, to give another example, was it magical or even edifying for a pianist of the stature of Ignaz Friedeman to be boycotted because he had included a Mendelssohn sonata in his programme – all Jewish and other non-Nordic forms of art having been officially revoked. But let that pass too, into the build-up of Nazi characteristics so spectacularly displayed at the Congress of Victory.

The ruthlessness of organization for example. Nearly half a million additional people had to be accommodated in and around a town whose normal population was no more than that. Discounting the 60,000 Hitler Youths who were distributed among ten huge marquees on a camping ground adjoining the Zeppelinwiese, the lower grades of Party members in serried rows of wood chalets like bathing huts, and the bigger fry who were put into hotels and guest houses, there were still some 300,000 to get into Nuremberg and its environs. This apparently afforded no problem. Factories, cinemas, churches, whole suburbs and villages were commandeered. Many Jews who ignored the red light burning so brightly and

Left: The friend. *Above:* The hero

failed to escape from the town during the months of preparation, were turned from their homes and stuffed into their Synagogue, where they lived as in a somewhat unsalubrious ghetto.

But as well as ruthlessness there was a truly astonishing industry displayed. More than ever before it was necessary to organize with the elaboration so characteristic of the Teutonic mind, leaving nothing to chance, fitting detail into detail. Improvisation would be considered direst inefficiency. Every eventuality was covered. One had only to turn to the instructions. For instance, the crew of a truck developing mechanical trouble in a convoy passing into the town had courses of action laid down to fit thirty-seven different sets of circumstances. These were indexed and cross-referenced so that no thought was needed – only obedience.

Obedience was also the keynote of the amazing efficiency with which huge gangs of workmen erected tents, marked roads for the motorcades, built barriers to keep the crowds in the right places, strengthened bridges, and constructed field kitchens; and, less spectacularly, worked out schedules, flagged on convoys, or heated thousands of gallons of soup to fortify the round-the-clock workers. From top to bottom of the hierarchy instant obedience was expected and received.

'An impressive number of *"Ja"*'s can be heard on all sides, the clicking of heels sounds like a fusillade, every site is riddled with Yes-men like woodworm, barking at each other with increasing fierceness as the lower orders are reached. But the huge wooden grandstand to hold 60,000 in the Luitpoldhain is up where only two days ago was nothing but a chalked-out space; hundred-foot towers topped with vast swastika flags stand like sentinels beside the stand and hundreds more thin flag-poles surround the arena. They say 1,500 pressmen can be got into the press box and 1,000 honorary guests on the main speakers' platform, which is as high as an ordinary house and reached by a golden stairway.'

So said the observer from the *Manchester Guardian.* He was right, not only in the statistical details but in his chilling reference to the omni-science of military conduct in civilian affairs.

Another reporter, from the staid London *Morning Post*, considered the financial backing needed for the enterprise.

'The world knows of Dr Alfred Hugenberg's financial support by way of the Nationalists and the German steel industry, and the Rhineland coal fields. Dr Schacht, lately President of the Reichsbank, and the industrialist Otto Wolf have been favourably enough inclined to the Nazis' aims to pull financial strings that have brought the Hamburg-Amerika shipping line to Herr Hitler's side also. Even so, the Nuremberg congress about to commence demonstrates the freedom with which money is spent, and there is a powerful feeling in Lombard Street that Herr Hitler has more money behind him than can be easily accounted for.'

All that was true. Even after the war, at the trials of the Nazi criminals when legal effort was being made to establish responsibility for the rise of the Party, it did not prove easy to trace its finances. But undoubtedly, huge sums came from German industry and possibly a certain amount was fed in from interested bodies abroad; also, dues from Party members amounted to a big total as the membership increased, and there was never any reluctance to squeeze every pfennig from every pocket by way of publications that were 'essential' reading, admission charges at public meetings, souvenirs such as the Party Day medals that formed badges of identity, and fines for non-attendance at Party activities. The organization

Songs of triumph

was as ruthlessly efficient in its finances as in everything else.

Arrogance: that too was part of the microcosm lavishly displayed. Streicher's extreme form was echoed in the swagger of Storm Troopers elbowing their way into crowded beer-halls, the new cry of *'Sieg Heil!'* and the strutting goose-step of troops marching through the town to their camping grounds. There was never any doubt in those narrow streets and winsomely picturesque squares of the forthcoming unfettered militarism.

Or of treachery either. Here during the spring Himmler worked at the plan for the purge of Storm Trooper leaders, the 'Night of the Long Knives' that would follow in just over a year and would bring more than a hundred 'conspirators' to their violent deaths during the weekend of 29th June – 1st July 1934. All of them – indeed the entire body of Storm Troopers – had been told by Hitler only a few months previously that 'every drop of his blood' would go to the defence of his oldest allies; and two of them, Ernst Röhm and Gregor Strasser, had helped Himmler to his place at the head of the Gestapo. Himmler unwaveringly accumulated and planted the 'evidence' of treason that would be used to justify the purge and the eventual eclipse of the Storm Trooper by the Gestapo.

Sycophancy too. Göbbels was by no means the only practitioner of that dubious ploy. Concentrated as the Party top- and under-dogs were at Nuremberg during the weeks of preparation for the Rally, there was endless jostling for privilege and position – the reverse, upward through the hierarchy, of the downward relay of the commands of the organization operatives. No stone was left unturned no avenue unexplored, no cliché unspoken in the solemn pursuit of crumbs of approval from the tables of the upper echelons. There was common sense in that. Approval was not merely an inflater of egos – it was a safeguard against the attention of

Himmler, so long as it did not become suspiciously sought.

These, then, were some of the facets of the 'complete microcosm of the Reich' noted by *Der Montag*.

As for the pageantry, the then current cinematic adjective 'epic' was justified. The splendours tried out at the 1929 affair were increased in number and organized into a more dramatically effective climax. Beginning, most appropriately considering that everything now was directed toward the ineluctable processes of war, with the sound of muffled drums, the events of the rally marched thunderously to their conclusion on 3rd September with a parade that lasted from noon until dusk, with countless thousands of Hitler Youth members marching past Hitler in battalions of 500 carrying a forest of swastika flags, every one of which was topped with the green oak leaves of victory. It was a parade without music, and most effectively, if surprisingly so. The only sound throughout the town was the incessant rhythmical beat of feet and the roar of the crowds. Simply in terms of endurance and volume it was impressive. 'Like a cup final in which a continual succession of goals is scored,' was one reporter's impression. The *New York Times* remarked with somewhat un-American meiosis, 'Young Germany was showing its strength.'

Between the muffled drums and the blaring fanfares announcing Hitler's arrival at the Deutscher Hof hotel at 8pm on 31st August, and that final threatening march through the town there came a series of spectacles and assemblies increasingly stimulating to the Nuremberg multitudes.

Even the less promising events were ceremoniously melodramatic. A thunderous ovation greeted the presentation of delegates from South America, the West Indies, Asia, Scandinavia, and Italy. Mussolini's Fascist representative was dressed from head to foot in black with a swirling black

Eagle designed by Speer

Party badge

Party-day medal 1929

Party-day medal 1933

Schellenbaum standard

Standard

Munich commemorative badge 1933

SS Standard-bearer's gorget

SS on parade

cloak and brought with him a falcon that sat, hooded, on his black gauntlet during the whole of a long pompous speech in which, in heavily accented German, he monotonously conveyed Mussolini's greeting. 'Il Duce reveres you,' he concluded, and marched off the platform to the oddly chosen music of *Il Bacio* played cumbrously on a euphonium. 'The disease [of Fascism] spreads,' the man from *Le Matin* dryly noted.

The presentation to Hitler of Dürer's engraving *Knight, Death and Devil* could not be left as a simple ceremony: it had to be supplemented by the projection of the picture on to a screen by epidiascope and a solemn lecture explaining it as symbolizing the great German battle against adversity and death. This too was greeted with tremendous applause.

But the really pompous pomp began on the morning of 1st September with the Consecration of the Flags. It

took place in the Congress Hall, where, to the sound of crêpe-draped muffled drums a uniformed SS man with skull-and-crossbones badge on his steel helmet slow-marched from entrance to platform through a tensely silent audience of 6,000. As he approached the platform the drums ceased and gave way to the recorded drums of the Berlin Philharmonic as they played the linking passage between the Scherzo and Finale of the Beethoven Fifth. He ascended the steps to the platform and turned to the audience to display the Blood Banner at the precise moment when the brass of the orchestra flared out in triumph.

The symphony concluded, the standard-bearers of all the new flags to be given the Nazi Host slow-marched to the platform for the consecratory touch while Ernst Röhm of the Storm Troopers read a roll of the names of those who had died for the Party. It would be dramatically

effective to add that his own name was included in the roll by mistake; and indeed some historians have been unable to resist that macabre touch; but there is no evidence to support it. Evidence or no, however, Röhm was already a man marked for murder because of his advocacy of the Storm Troopers as a body to supersede, rather than co-operate with, the army. Unfortunately for them, the Storm Troopers had become politically embarrassing to Hitler and he was anxious to rid himself of the effects of their reputation for thuggery and drunkenness. Their influence must be reduced. The Gestapo would be a much more reliable body. Himmler was very convincing on that score.

During the long ceremony of the roll call of the dead the audience stood in silence, many of them with tears streaming down their faces – an emotional outburst that bewildered many of the press representatives who were used to less demonstrative political gatherings. But they were as impressed as everybody else– which was of course the intention.

They had far more impressive sights to witness at the Zeppelinwiese next day. In the morning there was a parade of Party members – 160,000 of them – who were formed without the slightest hitch into phalanxes of 500 divided by wide avenues along which, to the sound of continual martial music played by massed brass bands, wave after wave of standard-bearers bore the forest of swastikas that would be seen again progressing through Nuremberg as the finale of the rally. One of the bandsmen gave Hamilton Burden, author of a book on Nuremberg, an eye-witness account of this morning review:

'At 6am we had to leave for the big meeting in the Stadium. We had to play for four hours from the speakers' platform to entertain the assembling formations while they were waiting. It was one of the most overwhelming sights to see from this high platform how the vast stadium filled slowly and very orderly with hundreds of thousands of uniformed men and women. In the field itself only uniformed

Hitler leaves the Luitpoldhalle after a speech

groups assembled, while huge crowds of civilians gathered on the side. Finally Hitler appeared with his staff. He sat down about six feet away from us. At this point I noticed the most interesting thing about this strange man. As he was sitting in front of us (it was by now about 9am and chilly rather than warm), I could see that Hitler began to sweat. He stared at the crowd which he could see but which could not see him yet. Slowly the back of his shirt began to discolour, a gradually growing dark spot began to show until his whole back was completely soaking wet. His apprehension seemed under control when he finally got up. We played the Crusaders' Fanfare and he began to address the crowds.'

The afternoon parade was of Hitler Youth, and their drilling was superb. After 60,000 of them had performed immensely complex formation exercises – 'Breathtaking in their marvellous co-ordination,' said the *Express* – they formed in the arena the living words *Blut und Ehre* (Blood and Honour) again and again, like aircraft signwriting, the beginning of the first

word fading as those at the rear of the serpentine column passed to its head to repeat Blood and Honour endlessly round the arena. Each one of them carried a long polished steel knife, and as a finale these were simultaneously drawn – 'to give the effect of a blinding flash in the high afternoon sun'.

The evening was crowned with another of Sauer's glittering firework displays, and it was scarcely over when at dawn began the move to the Luitpold arena for the commemoration service at the war memorial. That was heralded by the ringing of all the church bells of Nuremberg, and as it ended with the Horst Wessel song the Hitler Youth were already re-assembling for the final march past through the town that would end the pageantry of the rally in the early evening.

The speeches put into that three-day spectacular setting were as always doctrinal. Hitler, Rosenberg, Göbbels, Hess, Streicher, Feder (the Minister of Economics) all plunged into the usual fermenting diatribes against Marxism, democracy, the 'November criminals', international Judaism and its clutch on world economics, Weimar Versailles and the rest. From beginning to end of all the Nazi rallies the bludgeon never stopped bludgeoning. It was like an old grim joke that an old grim comedian endlessly repeats at every performance because he is always certain of having new members of the audience who will infect the others with their laughter however often the others may have heard it before. One can trace the course of Nazism solely from the inflection of the speeches made at the rallies. The targets were always the same and the assumptions were always the same. But this time, in 1933, the tone was different. Assurance had given them a more audibly rasping edge of attrition. The brazen fanfares of victory could be heard far beyond Nuremberg. The glint of knives could be seen as the sun set over Europe.

Full circle

That first rally of Nazis in the full flood of their power was filmed for public showing. Göbbels had recognized the propaganda value of the cinema as well as of broadcasting and had had no trouble in persuading Hitler to accept the establishment of both a film production unit and a film censorship bureau in the Ministry of Propaganda. Every film made in or imported into Germany had to be approved for its cultural value and

political harmlessness, which considerably reduced both output and imports, since someone on the viewing committee was almost certain to see something damaging to the Party in dialogue if not in plot. And if all else failed it was always possible to use the damning rubber stamp 'Worthless' *(Nichtssagend)*, which took care of a great deal.

However, since one of the Party's financial backers, Alfred Hugenberg, was also a backer of UFA, the biggest German film company, there was a malleable organization easily available to make pictures that were politically and culturally sound. There was also a talented director who had been an actress of star quality and had recently made a film, The Blue Light, that would become a classic of the cinema. (Two other films of

Hitler salutes the SS

Above: Torchlight parade.
Right: Banners by night.

hers have also become famously lodged in the repertory: SOS Iceberg and The White Hell of Pitz Palu.) Her name was Leni Riefenstahl. She was beautiful as well as talented, and Hitler, who fancied himself as a ladies' man, inveigled her into becoming official director of Party films. In an interview published in the *Saturday Evening Post* in 1946 she said that Hitler told her in 1932 that he intended to become leader of Germany – 'And when I am, I want you to make pictures just for me, just about me and the movement'. Which, from 1933 onward, she did.

So although there was no acceptable Reinhardt to put in charge of the production of each annual rally, there was at least a skilled movie maker on hand to record the pageantries for the benefit of those who could not get to Nuremberg, and for posterity.

Posterity reaped no benefit from Miss Riefenstahl's film of the 1933 rally. Having been made, its exhibition was banned and the original possibly destroyed, because of the purge killings of the 'Night of the Long Knives' when so many well known Party leaders like Röhm and Strasser, who naturally had appeared in the film, were murdered. It would have been foolish to remind the film's audiences of the risk Party members took in advancing the Nazi cause.

The 1934 film, though, was shown throughout Germany. The people were force-fed with it. It was compulsory showing in every cinema and school. The full version lasted three hours and it was euphemistically billed as a 'supporting' film, Göbbels blandly remarking that nobody had to see it but that, like owning a copy of *Mein Kampf*, to have seen it had definite value as proof of Party loyalty. Cinemas exhibiting it had the name of the film printed on the admission tickets, which the audience kept in case their loyalty was ever in doubt. Somewhat ironically in the circumstances the title was 'Triumph of the Will'.

It was an extremely well made film and Miss Riefenstahl even wrote a book about the making of it *(Hinter den Kulissen Reichsparteitagfilms)* describing her problems in lighting and directing it. She overcame them with remarkable ingenuity, and though the complete version is as tedious in its visual tautology as *Mein Kampf* is in the verbal kind, it is as impressive as the rally itself in its imagery and Germanic emphases. Like the town of Nuremberg, it bore the stamp of evil impressed upon it by Miss Riefenstahl's sensitive apprehension – which was not, incidentally, without mockery. The rhythmic marching in endless parades, the careful cutting to show every expression on the Führer's face

... and day

in accordance with mood and tempo, the shots of approaching convoys and multitudinous boots photographed from ground level ('Our motto shall be "If you will not be a German I will bash your skull in" '), and the great set pieces like the Consecration of the Flags and displays by the Labour Corps and Strength Through Joy organizations (which appeared for the first time in 1934) were seen to even greater advantage after going through the cutting-room. Not that they were anything but breathlessly effective in the actual performance. This was the rally that the American Foreign Correspondent William Shirer attended, and he wrote on 6th September, the third day:

'Hitler sprang his *Arbeitsdienst*, his Labour Service Corps, on the public for the first time today and it turned out to be a highly trained, semi-military group of fanatical Nazi youths. Standing there in the early morning sunlight which sparkled on their shiny spades, fifty thousand of them, with the first thousand bared above the waist, suddenly made the German spectators go mad with joy when, without warning, they broke into a perfect goose-step. Now, the goose-step has always seemed to me to be an outlandish exhibition of the human being in his most undignified and stupid state, but I felt for the first time this morning what an inner chord it strikes in the strange soul of the German people. Spontaneously they jumped up and shouted their

applause. There was a ritual even for the Labour Service boys. They formed an immense *Sprechchor* – a chanting chorus – and with one voice intoned such words as these: "We want our leader! Nothing for us! Everything for Germany! *Heil Hitler!*".'

And next night Shirer wrote:

'Another great pageant tonight. Two hundred thousand Party officials packed in the Zeppelinwiese with their 21,000 flags unfurled in the searchlights like a forest of weird trees. "We are strong and will get stronger" Hitler shouted at them through the microphone, his words echoing across the hushed field from the loud-speakers. And there, in the floodlit night, jammed together like sardines, in one mass formation, the little men of Germany who have made

Nazism possible achieved the highest state of being the Germanic man knows: the shedding of their individual souls and minds – with the personal responsibilities and doubts and problems – until under the mystic lights and at the sound of the magic words of the Austrian they were merged completely in the Germanic herd. Later they recovered enough – fifteen thousand of them – to stage a torchlight procession through Nuremberg's ancient streets, Hitler taking the salute in front of the station across from our hotel.'

And at the end of the last day of the rally, 10th September, (this was the first time the event had been scheduled to last a full week) he wound up his comments:

'Today the army had its day, fighting a very realistic sham battle in the Zeppelinwiese. It is difficult to exaggerate the frenzy of the three hundred thousand German spectators when they saw their soldiers go into action, heard the thunder of the guns, and smelt the powder. I feel that all those Americans and English (among others) who thought that German militarism was merely a product of Hohenzollerns – from Frederick the Great to Kaiser Wilhelm II – made a great mistake. It is rather something deeply engrained in all Germans. They acted today like children playing with tin soldiers. The Reichswehr "fought" today only with the "defensive" weapons allowed them by Versailles, but everybody knows they've got the rest – tanks, heavy artillery, and probably airplanes.

'Later. After seven days of almost ceaseless goose-stepping, speech-making, and pageantry, the Party rally came to an end tonight. And though dead tired and rapidly developing a bad case of crowd-phobia, I'm glad I came. You have to go through one of these to understand Hitler's hold on the people, to feel the dynamic in the movement he's unleashed and the sheer, disciplined strength the Germans possess. And now – as Hitler told correspondents yesterday in explaining his technique – the half-million men who've been here during the week will go back to their towns and villages and preach the new gospel with new fanaticism.'

And of course with the help of Miss Riefenstahl's film, Dr Göbbels' ceaseless propaganda via press, radio and hoarding, and Himmler's persuasive tactics via the Gestapo. (The Gestapo had been established as such, a force of secret State police with no pretensions to being a mere *corps d'élite* of body-guard troops, on 1st April 1934, and Himmler naturally was its head, with an almost equally unpleasant character Reinhard Heydrich, as his chief henchmen.)

'Triumph of the Will' was usually shown in an edited version that gained power by shortening. But just as the rallies themselves can be said to concentrate into a few days a microcosm of Hitler's power, so the film distilled the essence of all the rallies, past and future. Its long Wagnerian overture, opening shots of Nuremberg from the air, Hitler's plane descending, and miles-long columns of Storm Troopers closing in on the town establish at once the crude symbolism of power that persists throughout. Its very crudity is its most effective characteristic, and it is difficult to doubt that Miss Riefenstahl had her tongue slightly in her cheek, her sense of humour being somewhat keener than most of her compatriots'. But it was left to the British newsreel 'Movietone News' to parody 'Triumph of the Will' – in itself verging on a parody – in 'Germany Calling the Lambeth Walk', which by trick photography turned the rally film into a welcome joke for wartime audiences in Britain.

Streicher had offered the personnel making the film a large house, from which he had evicted a Jewish sculptor and his family, as their headquarters; and at the press reception given on

Street scene, Nuremberg 1937

Left: **Streicher leads the parade in memory of 9th November**
Above: **Nuremberg 1937**

4th September Göbbels presented him with the Ministry of Propaganda's 'Special Award for Co-operation'. It was a silver-mounted whip – the one that from now on he flourished as he strode through the town with his two Gestapo bodyguards.

By the time the 1935 rally was scheduled he had every reason for flourishing it with renewed viciousness – if indeed his viciousness could be said to need renewing. That was the year of the passing of the Nuremberg Laws. They were promulgated by Hitler at a session of the Reichstag held in the *Kulturvereinhaus* at 8 o'clock on the evening of Sunday 15th September, the penultimate day of the 1935 rally.

Göring presided, and a triumphant fanfare of trumpets followed his announcement that Hitler would now present to the Reichstag the new laws 'for the protection of German blood and honour'. They were the laws based on the 'five-point plan to diminish the influence of Judaism' worked out by Himmler eight years earlier. Though the penalties for breaking them did not include death, as had Himmler's original proposal, they could hardly have been more oppressive, more in keeping with the rule of a tyrant. They said, specifically, that German citizenship would in future exclude all Jews; that marriages between Jews and Germans were forbidden; that extra-marital relationships between Jews and German citizens were forbidden; that Jews were forbidden to employ German citizens under the age of forty-five as servants; and that Jews were forbidden to show or touch the national flag. The laws would be effective from midnight that night.

It was of course the first law that was the most evil. No Jew could now have any recourse to any kind of protection against persecution. They stood outside the State except as

149

subjects of derision and legalized terror – which, of course, from then on was unrelenting. The *New York Times* representative was subsequently expelled for publishing a report in his paper that read, in part:

'Gestapo visited the homes of between 300 and 400 Jewish families, mostly merchants and professional men, and confiscated bonds, check-books, savings bank books and savings found in houses. Only in a few cases were receipts given for the full or part of the confiscated values.

'Afterward the heads of the families in question were conducted to meeting places in town and from there to various sports places in the suburbs of Nuremberg. Some of the people were arrested in the streets or in shops, others during the morning services in the synagogue.

'Besides the moral torture and the objugations those several hundred men had to endure, some of them were beaten and scourged. Several were tortured with steel rods and dismissed only after they had signed a paper saying that nothing had happened to them.'

But the rally at which these permissive laws were passed and presented by Hitler as a gift to the German people, was as full of splendours as ever. 1935 was the year in which pretence was no longer sustained that · the ever-increasing German armed forces were merely 'defensive'. Wave after wave of tanks, armoured cars and mechanized artillery thundered across the arenas of the Luitpoldhain and the Zeppelinwiese in mock battles and elaborate formation displays. A hundred heavy bombers and as many fighter planes of the newly constituted Luftwaffe staged an air attack on a model village, and it was observed with delight by the vast crowds that both the attacking planes and defending anti-aircraft

Below: Nuremberg: a lighthearted moment: Göring and Hitler. *Right:* Hess's opening speech at the 1936 rally

batteries were superbly trained and phenomenally accurate.

In blessing the army at the end of its display with all the magnanimity of a pontiff, Hitler said:

'You are in war the nation's great defence, in peace the splendid school of our people. It is the Army which has made men of us all, and when we looked upon the Army our faith in the future of our people was always reinforced. This old glorious Army is not dead; it only slept, and now it has arisen again in you.'

Perhaps an appropriate phrase would be 'risen again with a vengeance'. By 1936 and the rally thematically concerned with 'Honour and Freedom' even its name had been changed from the simple 'German Army' (Reichswehr) to 'Armed force' (Wehrmacht). Naturally Hitler spoke of peace: 'We reject war for any purpose except to save the German nation's honour.' He had already, six months before the rally, marched 35,000 troops of the Wehrmacht into the demilitarized zone of the Rhineland without a tinkle of resistance from France. And now, in September, across the greatly extended arena of the Zeppelinwiese (it could now hold a quarter of a million men and 70,000 spectators) there moved in complex manoeuvres two regiments of cavalry, three battalions of infantry, four regiments of the Luftwaffe, a battalion of tanks, and sections of machine-gun and anti-aircraft troops. The sound and fury of this 'defence demonstration' as Hitler called it, brought the retrospective comment from Winston Churchill (in The Gathering Storm) that 'there was now . . . little hope of averting war or of postponing it by a trial of strength equivalent to war; . . . all that remained open to France and Britain was to await the moment of the challenge as best they could.'

The day before the army's field-day was given over to an equally significant parade. The New York Times man reported:

'Today's spectacle was calculated to

remain in the memory of all beholders. No country in Europe – it may even be said, no country in the world – could duplicate its significance, for it demonstrated the almost limitless reservoir of militant manhood, hardened and drilled and devoted to the point of fanaticism to Germany and the régime that rules it. Fifty-five thousand Storm Troopers, 20,000 SS men, 10,000 Motor Corps men, and 26,000 aviators from uniformed sports organizations outside the army formed the parading body. More than 10,000 additional Storm Troopers, standing shoulder to shoulder, lined the miles of streets through which they passed and kept back from the roadways the hundreds of thousands of spectators. All these men went on duty at 5 o'clock

Parade past Hitler's hotel,
Nuremberg 1937

in the morning. By 8 o'clock the street guards were in position and the paraders were massed on open ground adjoining the Zeppelin field and stadium. It was an impressive sight.'

Also impressive in its sophistry was Hitler's reply to those press men who asked him directly how close Germany was to re-arming for attack.

'I am highly amused by the suggestion,' he said, 'that these rallies at Nuremberg prove that Germany is mobilizing behind the camouflage of pageantry. The idea is absurd. There is no connection whatever between a gathering like this and the intention to send armed forces into aggressive battle.'

Not many other people were highly amused. Even such smiles as could be aroused on the faces of Allied statesmen were the hesitant smiles of discomfiture. Hitler's alliance with Mussolini was already clearly in the offing, as was the Anti-Comintern pact with Japan; the Spanish civil war had already begun and obviously was going to afford Hitler even greater advantages than Italy's invasion of Abyssinia; and in Britain the Baldwin government had adopted an attitude of cringing faith in the imposition of sanctions against Italy and in the old adage that to 'send a gunboat' to any scene of disturbance would make any political upstart quiver.

But not an upstart quivered. Hitler,

Torchlight parade

true, had had moments of apprehension after marching into the Rhineland: 'If the French had then opposed us,' he later said, 'we would have had to withdraw with our tails between our legs, for the military forces at our disposal would have crumpled against even a moderate resistance.' But bluff again served him well and his upper lip remained positively British in its unquivering stiffness.

Smiles far from hesitant flickered over the faces of some of the English and American reporters who covered the Labour Corps parade. The 50,000 men with their spades went through their complex choreography for nearly two hours, their movements and marching accompanied by massed brass bands and fanfares of trumpets. Then they divided into contingents and went through a strophic ceremony in which a *quasi* religious chanting went on, one contingent answering the other in earnest chorus:

'Once a year the spade shall rest. Once a year the day comes round when we must stand before our Führer and renew our faith.'
'Ready, O ready.'
'No one is too good –'
' – to labour for the Fatherland.'
'No one is too humble – '
' – to labour for the Fatherland.'
' To each the right and duty – '
' – to labour for the Fatherland.'
'We have carried you deep in our hearts but we cannot say it in words'
(*sic.*)

Social occasion: Nuremberg 1937

'Fatherland, Fatherland.'
'Duty is not serfdom. We carry the spade in the service of the nation.'
'Fatherland, Fatherland.'
'The Führer leads the world to peace.'
'And where he leads we follow.'

And so on. It was not unlike the steamier portions of Dr Göbbels' diary arranged for Greek chorus; but apart from those irreverent reporters who referred to it as 'the chanting of mindless yes-men' the 70,000 spectators were moved to deep emotion and indeed, like everything else at Nuremberg in rally time, there was a melodramatic grandiloquence about it that was impossible to fault if one considered its true purpose – which, again like everything else that Nuremberg stood for, was to continue relentlessly to project the Nazi image into the very heart of Germany. And, if one is to go by the *New York Times* correspondent of that and the succeeding years, into the world beyond too:

'At 8 o'clock a trumpet fanfare following a roar of cheers outside the arena announced Hitler's arrival. Then he appeared, a lone figure atop the wide steps at the far side of the arena. Awaiting him on the steps was a great gathering of high Nazi officials, all, like him, in brown uniform.

'As he appeared there shone upward from a hidden circle of 150 army searchlights behind the grandstands as many spears of light to the central point above.

'In this bright light Hitler walked down the steps through the group awaiting him and slowly, a procession with him at the head, marched across the field to the tribune. The thunderous cheers quite drowned the music of the great orchestras playing him in.

'He ascended the tribune and stood there waiting until there was complete silence. Then suddenly there appeared in the distance a mass of advancing red colour. It was the 25,000 red banners of Nazi organizations in all parts of Germany.

'The colour bearers marched with them across the rear of the brown columns on the field. Then they came forward, six abreast in the narrower lanes and twenty abreast in the wider centre aisle, so there was presented the spectacle of a great tide of crimson seeping through the lanes between the solid blocks of brown.

'Simultaneously the minor searchlights along the pillared rim above the grandstands were turned down on the field, lighting up the gilded eagles on the standards, so that the flood of red was flecked with gold. The effect was indescribably beautiful.'

Unlike the blackened heart and warped brain of the man whose image and megalomania were so colourfully projected. He had come a long way from the limp parish-pump meetings of the Party in Munich in 1919; a long way from the snow-sodden scene of the first rally in 1923. 'The Third Reich will last a thousand years,' he told the Hitler Youth at the 1937 rally, a few hours after he had consecrated the flags of the Gestapo, now a ubiquitous force with unlimited powers. And at the Reich Chancellery at Augsberg on 21st November 1937 he told the War Minister (Blomberg), the Army, Navy and Air Force chiefs (Fritsch, Raeder, Göring), and the Foreign Minister (Neurath):

'I am convinced that the most difficult part of the preparatory work has already been achieved. Today we are faced with new tasks, for the confines of our country are too narrow.'

Less than four months later, on 12th March 1938, Hitler's army marched over the German border into Austria. He had achieved the first extension of the confines of the country, restored to Germany the former heart of her great empire, his native land. And now – *Austriae est imperare orbi universo:* 'It is for Austria to rule the world'. Translated into 'Greater Germany' the theme of the last and greatest rally of all was already sounding brassily from the ramparts of tyranny.

Epilogue

The one-and-a-half million people departing from Nuremberg at the end of the 1938 rally and passing beneath the archway with its salutation 'Goodbye until 1939' left behind them a town intended as a shrine of triumph. 'I see Nuremberg as a city to which we shall yearly make a pilgrimage to give thanks for German victory over the forces of Versailles evil, the spreading cancer of the Jew, and Bolshevism.' Thus Hitler in his speech to the political leaders on the fifth day of the 1938 rally. But unfortunately for him and the monstrous doctrine of racial domination he had propounded and concentrated into the pageantry of the rallies for so long, he did not achieve anything to make a pilgrimage to Nuremberg for except the trials of his accomplices at the International Military Tribunal which began on 20th November 1945.

The indictment charged the defendants with responsibility for the deaths of twelve million men, women and children. The case for the prosecution was opened by Judge Robert Jackson who said that the crimes the tribunal sought to condemn had been so calculated, so malignant and devastating that civilization could not tolerate their being ignored because it could not survive their repetition. The trial, he told the court, represented the practical effort of four of the most mighty nations, with the support of fourteen more, to use international law to meet the greatest menace of the century – aggressive war.

'These twenty-two men facing the tribunal, and others who evaded it by taking their own guilty lives, created in Germany under the *Führerprinzip* a national socialist despotism equalled only by the dynasties of the ancient East . . . They led their people on a mad gamble for domination, diverted energies and resources to the creation of what they thought to be an invincible war machine, and invaded their neighbours to bring in millions of human beings as slave labourers. At last bestiality and bad faith reached such excess that they aroused the sleeping forces of imperilled civilization, which by its united efforts had ground the German war machine to fragments.'

Hitler had committed suicide on the afternoon of 30th April 1945; Göbbels on the evening of 1st May; Himmler after his arrest following the surrender of the German forces on the 7th. Göring faced his trial but took cyanide in his cell shortly before he was due to be hanged. Streicher faced his trial, was sentenced to death, and hanged with the remaining guilty Nazis on 16th October 1946, in Nuremberg.

Postscript

From the London *Times* 27th September 1969:

Nuremberg, Sept 26 – Police tonight banned the final election rally of Herr Adolf von Thadden, leader of the extreme right-wing National Democratic Party (N.P.D.) because public safety could not be guaranteed.

In spite of repeated drenchings from police water cannon, about 10,000 demonstrators, waving banners protesting against the N.P.D. filled the picturesque square where Herr von Thadden was to speak.

As the crowd swayed and surged across the cobbled square police behind barbed wire at the top of the hill opened up with five water cannon. The crowd was so dense that demonstrators at the front could do nothing to save themselves from a drenching as they were pushed forward by others at the rear.

Von Thadden's party followers fled, leaving behind their barbed-wire-encircled platform. About 1,000 police in white helmets ordered the rally banned to forestall violence. Then they told the demonstrators to go home.

But the anti-Thadden crowd set off firecrackers and met police charges with clubs, rocks and bottles.

Casualties came quickly – a bloodied girl was carried by police to an ambulance. Policemen, blood dripping from their hands, came stumbling from the battle to an emergency Red Cross first-aid station.

The battle of Egidien Square raged for more than two hours.

Later about 500 youths clashed with police in the centre of Nuremberg. Demonstrators streamed away from the square where the N.P.D. leaders were to have spoken, and marched with arms linked through the city.

Outside the main railway station, chanting, cheering youths scaled a 20-ft wooden N.P.D. campaign placard, tore it down and set it on fire. As it burned, police surged forward from lorries and charged into the stone-throwing crowd with truncheons.

Dr Horst Herold, the Nuremberg police president, said 21 policemen were injured in the clashes. Seven people received hospital treatment, four of them policemen. Three demonstrators were detained for resisting police but later released.

– Reuter.

Bibliography

The Story of Nuremberg Cecil Headlam (Dent, London)
The Nuremberg Party Rallies 1923-1939 Hamilton T Burden (Pall Mall, London. Praeger, New York)
Nazi Propaganda ZAB Zeman (Oxford, London and New York)
Mein Kampf Adolf Hitler translated by J Murphy (Hurst & Blackett, London)
Mein Kampf Adolf Hitler translated by R Manheim (Houghton & Mifflin, Boston)
Josef Göbbels Curt Riess (Hollis & Carter, London)
A New Social Philosophy Werner Sombat (Oxford, London. Princeton)
The House that Hitler Built Stephen H Roberts (Methuen, London)
Berlin Diary 1934-1941 William L Shirer (Hamish Hamilton, London)
The Nazi Seizure of Power William S Allen (Eyre & Spottiswoode, London. Quadrangle, Chicago)
Hitler: A Study in Tyranny Alan Bullock (Odhams, London and New York)
Germany's Revolution of Destruction Hermann Rauschning (Heinemann, London)
The Third Reich (Weidenfeld & Nicolson, London)
Nuremberg: The Unholy City Joshua Podro (Anscombe, London)
Germany's Third Empire Möller van den Bruck (Allen & Unwin, London)